Timeless Top 10 Travel Guides

London

London's Top 10 Hotel Districts, Shopping and Dining, Museums, Activities, Historical Sights, Nightlife, Top Things to do Off the Beaten Path, and Much More!

By Tess Downey

Foreword

London is one of the most popular tourist destinations in the world today- and with good reason. It isn't just the culture, the vibrant nightlife, the gorgeous parks, the amazing art and architecture, the historical monuments, or the flash, drama and music. It's the almost cliché of what we have come to expect of London - unrivalled in the world for its unapologetic celebration of what it is, what its history has made it, and what it has come to be in recent years.

A visitor to this magnificent city will be completely drawn in - just as soon as you step into its streets and mingle with the locals. Hear that accent? Notice those grey colors and the stormy clouds overhead? Armed with your London map, you wonder where to go. Perhaps the nearest castle, or the nearest royal park, or the museum they told you about, or maybe that cemetery from over a century ago.

Browse through these pages and pick one, two or all. Cross them off your list one at a time, and then come back again for more.

Table of Contents

Chapter 1: Introduction

People are flocking to London!

In 2013 alone, a record-breaking 16.8 million people visited London, and each year since - especially since the 2012 Olympics, the numbers just continue to grow. At recent count, some 31.5 million tourists came flocking to this UK capital in 2015.

Whether this is your first visit to London, or if this is one of several trips you have made to this metropolitan capital, there's always something new and different to see. Whether it's the history, the sights, the entertainment, the beer, or the people - a trip to London is always a worthy experience. There is something for everyone - whether you're a history buff, an outdoors person, someone fascinated by amazing art and architecture, or one interested in crime and the macabre - London is a unique mix of past and present jumbled together into a unique environment that is compelling as it is beautiful.

In this book, we present you with ten of the top attractions of each kind - whether it is museums and sights to see, historical attractions, outdoor places to explore, or quirky attractions that not all tourists know about - there is more than enough for the hungry tourist. Pack your bags, pack your umbrella, wear good and comfortable shoes, and let's set out for one of the most interesting places in the world.

A Brief History of London

It would be difficult to provide a summary of a history of London that is both brief and yet comprehensive - a history that spans over 2,000 years of grandeur, drama, tragedy, and victories. And yet one does need to delve into a bit of London history to fully appreciate the sights and attractions of this now-bustling metropolitan city.

Below is a brief timeline of some of the notable events of London's past - tracing its development until present times:

- 50 AD - the Romans founded the first major settlement along the River Thames, which they called Londinium
- 61 AD - Iceni Queen Boudicia led a rebellion against the Romans, and Londinium was razed by fire and destroyed. It was quickly rebuilt after the Romans stomped out the rebellion.
- 180-225 AD, the defensive London Wall was built by the Romans around the landward side of the city. This would define the perimeters of the City of London in the centuries to come.
- 5th century - Decline of the Roman Empire, and the Roman occupation of Britain ends. Londinium declined, and was virtually abandoned.
- 6th century - Saxons created a trading settlement at Covent Garden, outside the Roman walls. Population is estimated to have grown to some 10-12,000 people.
- Early 7th century - London became incorporated into the kingdoom of the East Saxons, the first post-Roman bishop Mellitus was appointed. St. Paul's Cathedral was founded.
- 650 - Christianity was permanently established in the East Saxon Kingdom, including London.
- 9th century - Vikings attacked London several times, and sacked several times, in 842 and 851.
- 871 - The Danish "Great Heathen Army" wintered in London, in whose hands the city remained until 886,

when it was captured by King Alfred the Great of Wessex. The city was renamed Lundenburh, and focused mostly on defensive fortifications, and a second fortified Borough was established on the Southbank at Southwark.

- 978 - The City of London grew in commercial and political importance.
- 1013 - Viking attacks resumed, and London fell. King Æthelred fled abroad. His son Edmund Ironside was proclaimed king in 1016. After his defeat at the Battle of Assandun, Edmund ceded all England north of the Thames to Norse King Cnut the Great, who had control of the entire country after Edward's death a few weeks later.
- 1042 - Cnut's dynasty ended, and English rule was restored under Edward the Confessor. Westminster Abbey was founded. Edward left no heirs however, and there followed a succession dispute.
- 11th century - Norman conquest of England, and William the Conqueror is crowned king of England. The Tower of London is built.
- 1176 - London Bridge is built, and remained the only bridge across the River Thames until 1739.
- 1216 - the First Barons War, when Prince Louis of France is acclaimed King of England. He later withdrew from England after his supporters rallied around Henry III and the House of Plantagenet.

French influence is gradually shaken off in the succeeding centuries.

- 1381 - The Peasant's Revolt, when London is invaded by rebels and the Tower of London is stormed and the city looted. The revolt collapsed after the death of its leader, Wat Tyler.
- Mid-14th century - The Black Death strikes in three succeeding waves, and London loses over half of its population.
- 1530-1538 - Henry VIII's Dissolution of the Monasteries.
- 1603 - Under Tudor reign, London grew as an important commercial centre in Europe. Trade expanded to Russian, the Levant, India, and the Americas; the period of monopoly trading companies such as the British East India Company. Immigrants came to settle in London, and its population swelled to about 225,000 in 1605.
- late 16th to early 17 century - flourishing of drama, and William Shakespeare as a preeminent figure.
- 17th century - London expanded beyond its original boundaries. The dissolved monastery of Charterhouse is converted into Charterhouse School, a principal public school in London. Another plague epidemic strikes Lonon in 1665.
- 1666 - The Great Fire of London. The city was later rebuilt along much of the same lines that it follows

today. Stone and brick buildings were preferred over wooden construction to reduce the risk of fire. St. Paul's Cathedral was rebuilt.

- 17th century - London became an important trading capital, imported and then re-exported throughout the rest of Europe and the world. This was followed by the construction of several important buildings such as Kensington Palace, Greenwich Hospital, Westminster Bridge, Chelsea Hospital, and various churches outside the City of London.
- 1750 - Crime rate increased, and the Bow Street Runners were established as a professional police force. Public hangings were common and popular public events.
- 1760 - The beginnings of the Industrial Revolution, which lasted to sometime between 1820 to 1840.
- 1763 - Britain emerged as a leading colonial power after victory in the Seven Years' War.
- 1780 - The Gordon Riots, uprising by Protestants against Roman Catholic emancipation. Catholic churches and homes were damaged.
- 1801 - Increasing influx of tradesmen and immigrants, and the population swelled to about 950,000. Markets expanded, trade increased, boosting London's prosperity.
- 18th century - breakaway of American colonies, and the age of Enlightenment.

- 19th century - London became the world's largest city, and the capital of the British Empire. It was also a city of contrasts - wealth and poverty together, which Charles Dickens immortalized in his novels. The railway system was also put in place, and the wealthier of the population emigrated to the suburbs. Most of the inner city areas were inhabited by the poorer class.

- 1858 - the Great Stink of 1858, which led to the constructed of a large sewerage system. Prior to this, sewage was pumped straight into the River Thames. Clean drinking water was also safeguarded. As a result, the death toll dropped, and so did epidemics of cholera and other diseases. This sewerage system is still in use today.

- 1845-49 - large influx of immigrants into London, including Catholic Irish who were fleeing from the Great Famine, and also a large Jewish community.

- 1888 - new County of London was established, and London was subdivided into 28 metropolitan boroughs.

- 20th century - London's population continued to expand, and public transport also expanded - including a large tram network, a motorbus service, and improvements to the rail network.

- WWI - London was bombed by air raids carried out by German zeppelin airships.

- 1930s - the Great Depression, and severe unemployment. By 1939, London's population had reached up to 8.6 million.
- 1940-1941 - the Blitz, and the bombing of London during WWII. Many historic buildings were destroyed. This continued during 1944-1945, known as the little Blitz. The city was devastated, over 30,000 people killed, thousands of buildings destroyed, and hundreds of thousands of people left destitute and homeless.
- 1950s-1960s - tower blocks were built, offering high-rise flats as an answer to the housing problem. The Great Smog of 1952 killed over 4,000 people - coal-produced smoke which lasted for 5 days. After this, the Clean Air Act of 1956 was passed.
- mid-1960s - London was a centre of international youth culture (the Swinging London subculture), owing to the popularity of groups such as the Beatles and The Rolling Stones.
- 1950s to mid 1990s - London became a diverse city with the arrival of huge numbers of immigrants from different countries. Tensions escalated, leading to various conflicts such as the Brixton Riots in the early 1980s, and attacks from the Provisional IRA from the 1970s until the mid 1990s.
- 1965 - the area of London was expanded to include 32 new London boroughs, now called Greater London.

- 21st century - in preparation for the new millenium, various modern projects were instituted, such as the construction of the London Eye and the Millenium Bridge, and some of the historical monuments were enhanced, such as the roof of the Great Court of the British Museum. In 2012, London hosted the Olympics and Paralympics.
- At present, the population of Greater London is estimated to be upwards of 8 million. Although now larger in scope, area, and population, much of its commerce remains the same as in Roman times: a center of trade and commerce, though of course it has now grown to one of the largest in the world.

Chapter Two: Hotels and Accommodations

How do you pick out the best place to stay in London? This isn't the easiest question to answer. For one thing, it is estimated that there are about 123,000 hotel rooms in Greater London in 2010, and more than 70,000 three to five star hotel rooms within 10 kilometers of Central London in 2003.

For another, they may not always be cost-friendly. Reviews from back in 2011 have ranked London Hotels as the 8th most expensive hotels in the world, and more recently, or in February 2015, London was considered the most expensive city in Europe in terms of the advertisted hotel rates.

So we have put together this list of what we consider to be the top 10 best hotel districts in London. Some are very expensive, while others are a bit more cost-friendly. The variety of hotel accommodations you can probably expect may include any of the following:

- Hostels
- Bed & Breakfast
- Budget Hotels (2-3 star ratings)
- 4 Star Hotels
- 5 Star Hotels

- Apartments for short-term lease
- Rooms for rent
- Family Rooms for rent

Altogether, these present the traveler with a wide range of diverse hotels to choose from, all of which would hopefully provide you with a place to stay that is also, at the same time, a bit of traveling experience, too.

1. West End

London's West End is generally considered to be the main commercial and entertainment center of the city. It is the largest central business district in London and in the

United Kingdom, and is also a pretty expensive location to put up for the night.

If expense is not a factor for you, this is a great place to choose a hotel if you're aiming to visit London's art galleries and museums, or to watch one of West End's theatrical performances. And aside from a wide range of shops in the nearby vicinities, you will also have easy access to various entertainment spots: aside from theatres, there are cinemas, nightclubs, bars and restaurants. And to take a an outdoor break, there is Hyde Park corner, Covent Garden and Soho, Mayfair, Trafalgar Square, Marble Arch, Oxford Street Shopping, and Piccadilly Circus. Nearby places of note to explore include the British Museum, Theatreland, the British Library, Dickens House Museum, and various historic buildings and streets. Most of the hotels, which are 4 or 5 star hotels, are located around the Marble Arch at the Western end of Oxford Street.

On the downside, it may be a bit difficult getting to this area from the airport. But Paddington Station is near, with available trains to Heathrow. There are also direct airport buses to Stansted and Luton airports.

2. Bloomsbury

If you want convenient access to West End's tourist spots, stores and boutiques, or the lively entertainment and theatrical shows, but still would like to save a bit more in terms of your hotels and accommodations, the Bloomsbury district is a good option. This is still an expensive district for hotel accommodations - of which there is a wide variety to choose from, but slightly cheaper in rates compared to West End.

One can also easily walk to West End and take advantage of the entertainment, galleries and shops there. Bloomsbury also offers a good choice of bookshops, shops offering an assortment of curios, and quirky attractions. The British Museum and Covent Garden are pretty near, and many schools, universities and hospitals are located here. Bloomsbury also features fine parks and squares, such as Russell Square, Bedford Square, Bloomsbury Square, and Tavistock Square.

One can easily get here from any airport or cruise port, though te only direct link is London Underground to Heathrow, which is about 15 miles distant. There are three Underground stations that open right onto Bloomsbury, including those on Russell Square, King's Cross St. Pancras, and Euston Square. All in all, it is a good and convenient place to begin a tour of the rest of London.

3. *County Hall and Waterloo*

This area of Waterloo in Lambeth is more commonly known for the landmark County Hall, which sits on the south Bank of the River Thames. The area is rife with businesses and attractions, including many developments by Merlin Entertainments such as the London Eye, London Sea Life Aquarium, and the London Dungeon. Other nearby places of interest include Big Ben and the Palace of Wesminster, Westminster Abbey, all the way to Trafalgar Square. This is mainly a government area, and entertainment centers such as night clubs or bars are not common. Mainly, this is a good spot for those who want to do some sightseeing. Room rates are cheaper during weekends, which makes it an attractive option.

There is a diverse selection of hotels in this area, some luxury hotels such as the Marriott Hotel, but there you also have options for budget accommodations. The fastest route to get to his area is by bus; it is accommodated by Underground Stations, but none direct.

4. Victoria

Victoria is a small district in Westminster in Central London, and its main central hub is the Victoria Train Station. Millions of people pass through Victoria each year, and so its hotel district is also one of London's largest. Commuting from here should be fairly easy, as it is also a major hub for transport vehicles such as bus and taxi services. It's a very convenient area for those flying into Gatwick.

Expect to see a lot of fellow tourists in this area, as there are a lot of available budget accommodations, though be aware that they may be sold on during weekends, when room rates are cheaper. If you intend to find accommodations in this area - where it is close to Buckingham Palace and the Changing of the Guards, you may want to book your rooms early on.

5. *City of London*

The City of London is both a city and a county that is situated within the Greater London metropolis. It is located within central London, and is sometimes referred to only as "the City." It comprises mostly of the area wherein the original Roman settlement is located - up until London's development in the Middle Ages. So in a very real way, the City of London "is" London.

The City continues to be a major business and financial centre - Lloyd's building and insurance businesses to the east, and outside of the City, at Canary Wharf. The area has a rich commercial district - with insurance companies, banks, the London Stock Exchange, and trading. While only around 7,000 people reside in the City of London, an estimated 300,000 commute to and from the City for work. The Inns of Court are also located here - in Temple and Chancery Lane.

The City's tourism is therefore focused mainly on the business elite - and this is reflected in their prices. If you are traveling on a budget, or if you have a large family with kids, this area might not be convenient, or relaxing for you. Most of the landmarks here include historic churches - this would be a good place to stay if this is what you came to see. Travelers might find it better to come to the City during weekends though - when the businessesmen and women have gone home, and hotel rates have dropped. There are a number of hotels near the Tower of London, and they are diverse enough to offer you a choice between 4 star hotels or budget accommodations.

Other landmarks include St. Paul's Cathedral, the Tower of London and Tower Bridge, the Globe Theatre, Tate Modern, and Borough Market. In recent years, riverside warehouses have made way for bars and restaurants, so there is more in the way of entertainment, too.

There are two stations - London Bridge and Liverpool, and they have direct trains to Gatwick, Stansted, and Luton Airports. Heathrow Airport, on the other hand, is not recommended if this is your intended location.

6. King's Cross

King's Cross is located north of Charing Cross Station, and is probably most identified with one of its railway stations - King's Cross Railway Station. This is actually one of the major railways entering London from the north.

Originally known as Battlebridge, this was the site of the famous battle between the Romans and the local Iceni tribe led by Boudica. In fact, there is a local urban folklore that Boudica is buried between a platform at King's Cross Station. Its current name, however, derives from King George IV's monument that was built at a crossroads in the area that is now Euston Road. This was a sixty feet high statue that, at the time, cost no more than £25. This was demolished in 1845, however, and a Lighthouse Building built in its place. The name, however, was retained.

Near this very junction, in fact, is where King's Cross Railway Station currently stands. St. Pancras is to the west. The area was known for fish, coal, potatoes and grain, but after WWII, its economy degenerated, and it was notorious for being a prostitution and drug area. It took some time before King's Cross can be revived and to move past this public perception.

Today, there is a healthy and thriving economy, and King's Cross is known for its various cultural establishments. Redevelopment is still expected to continue in the next few years, and already work on the King's Cross Central is underway.

This is a great place to find affordable hotels, bed and breakfasts, and hostels - some of them conveniently located near King's Cross Station. There is also a good selection of some 3 and 4 star hotels, and there is the 5 star Renaissance Hotel St. Pancras. A good place for tourists on a budget. It is relatively quiet in terms of the night scene, and places to see include the British Library and Camden Market. But it's a good area to use as a home base in exploring the rest of London, as there are direct train links to Heathrow, Gatwick, and Luton, and to the Dover cruise port.

Here's one interesting trivia: at King's Cross Station, where J.K. Rowling's Harry Potter boards the train for Hogwarts, a sign has actually been put up for Platform 9 3/4, and a luggage trolley is buried halfway into the wall.

7. *Kensington*

Kensington is located in west London, within the Royal Borough of Kensington and Chelsea. Some of the landmarks of the area are Kensington Gardens, the Albert Memorial, Speke's monument, and the Serpentine Gallery.

Commerce mainly revolves around Kensington High Street, which is also the location for the Royal Albert Hall and the Royal College of Music. There are many upmarket shops along this street, and it is generally considered to be one of the best among London's shopping districts. A few more medium-sized shops are located in South Kensington.

Kensington caters to the affluent. While there are some cheaper accommodations farther west and close to Earls' Court, the eastern side of this area has some of the most exclusive and high budget hotels in London. One notable thing about Kensington is that despite its booming economy, it has so far resisted the influx of too many high rise buildings. Instead, its residents have taken to subdividing large, mid-rise Georgian and Victorian terraced houses. It's an ideal location for shot-let apartments.

The landmarks here are also, in a way, high brow: V&A Museum, Royal Albert Hall, Albert Memorial in Hyde Park, Kensington Gardens, Harrods, the Natural History Museum, the Science Museum, and the Royal College of Music. And of course, Kensington Palace, where Prince William and Kate reside. It's a great place to troop through the museums in the area, and to simply enjoy the sights.

This is a very convenient location if you are using Heathrow Airport.

8. *Bayswater*

Bayswater is a district located within the City of Westminster and the Royal Borough of Kensington and Chelsea, right within central London.

This is a melting pot of cultures: English, Arab, Greek, Moscow, French, Americans, and Brazilians. Bayswater's population is dense, and there is also a high concentration of hotels, boarding houses, apartments and flats in this area. Prices range from very expensive to midrange to cheap - though you do get what you pay for. If you manage to find a good hotel, this can be a very pleasant place to stay at. One good effect of the mixture of cultures in this area is a great variety of ethnic cuisine restaurants along Queensway, the main High Street, which tourists will have fun exploring.

This district borders Hyde Park, and is near Kensington Palace, Hyde Park, Portobello Market, and Notting Hill. It is also near Paddington, and therefore a good choice for those using Heathrow.

9. *Paddington*

Also located within central London, Paddington is an area within the City of Westminster, and was integrated with Greater London in 1965.

Historically, Paddington was a part of Middlesex, and it was speculated that they were Saxon settlements near the intersection of Roman-built roads. There was a time, too, when the area was known for the public executions that were conducted at the Tyburn gallows - at a junction that is now known as Marble Arch. Locals have since developed the district, and since then it was known for being an elegant, prosperous and respectable district.

Today, much work is being done on a project called Paddington Waterside, that is targeted to finish by 2018, and there have been many new developments since the project was begun in 1998. It is also the location of St. Mary's Hospital, and the Paddington Green Police Station - said to be the most important high-security police station in the UK. Other notable landmarks here are Hyde Park, Little Venice, Regent's Park, and the Sherlock Holmes Museum.

The neighborhood is a quiet and family-friendly area; there is a diversity of accommodations, many budget friendly, though there are some 4 star hotels. There isn't much of a night life to speak of, but

The Paddington Railway station is a very busy place, with thousands of commuters passing through every day. It is the terminus for the Heathrow Express train to Heathrow, and for trains to the west of England and Wales.

10. Canary Wharf

Canary Wharf lies to the east of the center of London, and is one of London's main financial districts. Together with the City of London, it is one of the traditional financial centres in the UK. If your trip to London includes business as well as pleasure, and maybe a visit to one of the many financial centers in this area, this might be a convenient location for you. There are also numerous hotel accommodations available on Canary Wharf - though expect these to be a bit pricey.

The area - formerly the West India Docks - was completely rebuilt after it was closed in the 1980s. All its buildings are, therefore, quite new. It caters mainly to the business and working class, and houses many of Europe's major banks, professional service firms, and media organizations. Around 105,000 people work here, and the area also provides numerous restaurants, bars, shopping and leisure facilities - most of them high end.

Hotel options are also of the luxury type - featuring large chains of global hotel names.

Canary Wharf is located on the West India Docks on the Isle of Dogs, and may be reached by the Jubilee Line of the London Underground, or any of the slower river boat services.

Another possible option is a few miles east - and the hotels around the redeveloped dock around the City Airport and the Excel Exhibition Centre. This is also an expensive area, but comparatively, are slightly cheaper than Canary Wharf.

Chapter Three: Shop and Dine in London

One of the best ways to truly get to know a place you're visiting is to explore some of their local shops, and to try out their local cuisine. Not only does this bring you in closer touch with the locals, but you also have a fun and memorable experience of exploring the local shopping and dining hubs.

It would be difficult to present you with a list of specific shops and restaurants to try out - there are literally thousands of them in London, and what you will shop for will depend on what you're looking for, or where you find yourself ending up in your explorations. So instead, this chapter presents you with ten of the best loved and most popular shopping and dining districts in London - and with a short description of what you might expect in each area - we leave you on your own to explore.

It's always a good idea to know what you're intending to buy when you go out for a day of shopping; at the same time, make it a habit to be open to whatever unexpected delight crosses your path. And when you enter the next restaurant near the corner to fill your growling stomach after a hard day of shopping, be open to whatever tastes and flavors you will find, and remember to tip generously if they end up exceeding your expectations.

1. Regent Street

Regent Street is one of the foremost shopping destinations in London. Located in the West End of London, it is lit up beautifully every Christmas. It was originally named after the Prince Regent, George IV, and features some beautiful Georgian architecture. The entire street cuts through several locations of note in London, running from Carlton House (which was the Regent's residence), through Piccadilly Circus and Oxford Circus, all the way to All Souls Church.

It is home to more than 75 international flagship stores, such as Apple, Liberty, Banana Republic, J. Crew,

Karl Lagerfeld, Burberry, Penhaligon's, Anthropologie, Hamley's, and COS. Regent Street also features a great number of stylish cafes, restaurants and bars. Heddon Street (Tibits, Aubaine, Gaucho and Momo), Swallow Street (Fishworks and Freggo) and The Quadrant (Whole Foods Market, Cafe Royal and Tonic) provide the shoppers temporary respite from all the bustle of shopping and offer places to relax, eat and drink.

Regent Street generally opens at 10 am and closes from 8 to 9 pm, though many of the restaurants and bars are still open until late. They also have a handy app that can be downloaded from the Apple app store, which gives one a ready-at-hand historic guide to the beautiful and historic Regent Street.

2. *Knightsbridge*

Knightsbridge is an exclusive residential and retail district in West London, but did you know that for centuries, it was once associated with highwaymen, robbers and cutthroats? Today, any crime committed along Knightsbridge would be a high-profile crime, simply because this is a seriously expensive place to live, to shop and to dine.

Perhaps one of the most famous landmarks of Knightsbridge is Harrods, the most popular and largest local department store in London. Those with money to burn, however, avoid the crowds and Harrods and prefer Harvey Nichols. On Sloane Street, you can also find some designer shops such as Christian Dior, Cnahel, Gucci, Armani, Prada,

Alberta Ferretti, Nicole Fahri, and Katharine Hamnett. You can try shopping for antiques in Alfie's Antique Market - the largest covered antique market in London; explore cookware at Divertimenti, sunglasses at Cutler and Gross; designer bags at Anya Hindmarch, or famous designer shoes from Christian Louboutin.

Tired from all the shopping? Knightsbridge also features delectable places to eat such as The Hummingbird Bakery, Rococo Chocolates Belgravia, Baker & Spice, and Patisserie Valerie. There is also a fifth floor cafe at Harvey Nichols. If it's a meal you're looking for, look no further than Dinner by Heston Blumenthal, Indian restaurant Haandi, Hawksmoor, Koffman's, Marcus, the Bar Boulud in Mandarin Oriental, and the hip bar and restaurant Zuma. Other places to try are Toto's, Rivea, and Petrus.

3. *Covent Garden*

Covent Garden lies on the eastern fringes of West End, between St. Martin's Lane and Drury Lane. It used to be known for its fruit and vegetable market in the central square, and it still features the Covent Garden Market, among many other shops, pubs and bars, restaurants, and even street performances that have since sprung up in the area. Visiting Covent Garden means a total immersion into the rich cultural and historical life of England, as befits what was once a bustling Anglo-Saxon trading town.

Covent Garden has its own distinctive landmarks, including the Royal Opera House, the Covent Garden Market, the Theatre Royal on Drury Lane, The London Transport Museum, St. Paul's Church, and the incomparable Covent Garden Square - a beautiful covered square with

French and Italianate design influences, and where one will find the area's colorful street performers.

There are over 60 pubs and bars in Covent Garden, a wide range of restaurants such as Rules, J. Sheekey, The Ivy, Gaby's Deli, Clos Maggiore, Mon Plaisir, Flat Iron Henrietta Street, and Belgo Central. There is also a fine selection of coffee shops available in the area, some of them among London's earliest coffee shops.

4. Oxford Street

Oxford Street is generally considered to be London's, and Europe's busiest shopping district - so much so that pedestrianization (and the restriction of traffic) was attempted several times in order to help with decongestion. Regardless of which traffic policies are currently being adopted, however, Oxford Street remains a very popular and in demand retail area, with several big names such as Selfridges, John Lewis, HMV, and Topshop.

Interestingly, what was once known as Oxford Road was far more notorious - it was the steet where Newgate prisoners passed on their way towards a public hanging. It eventually evolved from a residential to a commercial district, but and attracted a diverse subset of the population: it was known for being a haunt of prostitutes, conmen, and street traders.

Today, it is a primary London shopping and retail area, and is still estimated to draw around a million visitors daily. If you don't mind rubbing shoulders with a wide cross section of London's population, this is a very interesting place to go to shop, to dine, to have coffee, or to sit down and have a pint in one of the area's many bars.

5. Carnaby Street

Carnaby Street is a pedestrianized shopping district in Soho, in the City of Westminster in Central London. One recognizes Carnaby Street by its distinct archway, and is located just a few minutes' walk away from Oxford Circus and Piccadilly Circus tube stations. There are more than 30 independent stores and boutiques, among then some popular flagship stores. In fact, Carnaby Street was once world-famous as a hot spot in Swinging London during the 60s - catering to youth and revolution, fashion and industry, and lifestyle retailers. Back then, it was the second most popular tourist destination in London - after Buckingham Palace.

Today, Carnaby Street retains much of its youthful energy and trendy vibe. Its 13 streets are famous for their trendy fashion boutiques and global brands, making it one of London's most distinctive and popular shopping districts.

Oxford Street also features the Kingly Court - a food hub in a three-storey building, with more than 20 places to sample. Try out Le Bab , Señor Ceviche, Dirty Bones Pizza Pilgrims, and the Detox Kitchen.

6. *King's Road*

King's Road was literally once the King's Road - that is, King Charles II's private road between Whitehall and Hampton Court Palace. It was a symbol of "mod culture" during the 60s, and is the site of the UK's first branch of Starbucks - back in 1999.

It offers visitors a diverse range of shops and dining places: there are many shops for the fashion-hungry, such as Jigsaw, French Connection, Benetton, American Classics, Ben de Lisi, Ellis Street, Emma Hope, and even Vivine Westwood's first ever store. There are also smaller, independent shops that one can visit as one walks towards the west, and away from Sloane Square. The area also offers a good selection of contemporary furnishing stores and inspiration interior design - if you can't find what you're looking for at Chelsea Antiques Market. This is a great place to buy those souvenirs!

For places to eat, you can try the Top Floor of Peter Jones, Patisserie Valerie, or Manicomio Restaurant. There's also Gallery Mess, The Five Fields, and Rasoi. King's Road also offers a wide selection of pubs such as The Phoenix, The Orange Public House, and The Admiral Codrington, among others.

7. *Broadway Market*

Broadway Market runs from London Fields to the Regent's Canal in Haggerston, in the London Borough of Hackney in the east of London. It used to be a fruit and vegetable market, but in recent years, it has slowly diversified and now offers a wide range of consumables - from vintage clothing, eclectic foods, arts and crafts, and their original products: fresh produce.

The site was built on an old drover's root into the city, and while it was an active market for fruits and vegetables since the 1890s, its commercial activities slowly dwindled over time. By 2000, there were only a couple of stalls along the street that sold produce.

It wasn't until 2004 when volunteers and local residents' associations actively set about to transform the ailing fruit and vegetable market into what it is now - one of the most popular and successful London market.

There are over 80 stalls selling everything from fish, meat, cheese, cakes, preserves, and of course, fruits and vegetables. Independent shops have also opened up, selling clothing and arts and crafts, while pubs, restaurants and cafés dot the street scene. Many of the cake and delicacies sold by the different stores are widely appreciated by visitors.

For a wide selection of clothes, try Geoffrey J. Finch and the label Antipodium, Artwords; café Climpson & Sons, The Dove, and Wilton's are great places to recharge and refuel; and for interior decorating and vintage furniture, try Arch 389 and The Dog and the Wardrobe.

8. *Camden Town*

Camden Town started out as Camden Place, and was named after Charles Pratt, the 1st Earl of Camden. Camden was the name on the Ordnance Survey map in 1822, and was later applied to the Camden Town Group of artists, as well as the London Borough of Camden, sometime in the early 20th century.

Camden Town is an inner city district of London, and is one of 35 major centres that were identified in the London Plan for the Greater London area in 2004. It was originally earmarked as a residential district, but became increasingly identified with the Camden markets in 1973. In time, the area's retail and industrial economy grew, and is a prime location for service industries, while also hosting street markets and music venues. Overall, Camden Town is strongly associated with alternative culture.

There's actually a lot to see and do in Camden. For one thing, it has a number of interesting historic places, such as The Camden Eye (an old prison), St. Michael's Church, the Carreras Cigarette Factory, Bedford Music Hall, and the Jewish Museum. Camden Town was also the home of some significant people such as Charles Dickens (his second London home), boxer Tom Sayers, Beryl Bainbridge, poet Dylan Thomas, and singer Amy Winehouse, among others.

Camden Markets nowadays provide the visitor with a real mix of shopping options: from goth and punk clothing to Doc Martins, tattoos and body piercings. There are plenty of stores that sell vintage-everything - clothes, accessories, and even boutiques. Explore Camden Lock Market, Camden Lock Village, Camden Market, Inverness Street Market, and Stables Market.

Regent's Canal runs along the heart of Camden and it markets, and it is a literal Little Venice through which you can take a boat tur. There are live performances from various renowned artists, and with its wide selection of pubs, bars and live music venues, Camden Town has a lively nightlife.

And finally, don't forget to sample some of their food - the Roundhouse, Trufflesecco, Masala Zone, Q Grill, Shaka Zulu, York & Albany, Gilgamesh, Poppies, or try any of the wide variety of food stalls at Camden Lock Market.

9. Bond Street

For a bit more of an elegant touch, you can try Bond Street - an area famously known for designer fashion and luxury goods.

Set in historic Mayfair - the place to be for the upper class residents of Mayfair; the most stylish, wealthiest and the most influential people - since the end of the 18th century, prestigious and expensive shops have since proliferated on Bond Street.

A visit to Bond Street is a combined treat of traditional elegance and modern luxury - prestige itself rolling off some of the names of retailers and haute couture stores such as Burberry, Chanel, Cartier, Dolce Gabbana, Jimmy Choo, Louis Vuitton, Ralph Lauren, Bulgari, Asprey and Tiffany. To this day, it is a haunt of celebrities, socialities, and the international jet set.

Enjoy some of Bond Street's unique landmarks such as The Royal Academy of Art, Sotheby's, and even the popular "Allies" statue of Winston Churchill and Franklin D. Roosevelt sitting on a park bench engaged in conversaton together.

There are also a number of great restaurants around or near Bond Street, such as Bond & Brook, Mayfair Pizza, Joe S Restaurant Bar, Cartizze, Hush Mayfair, La Petite Maison, Goodman, and Little Social, among others.

10. *Westfield Shopping Centre*

Westfield is a shopping centre name owned by the Westfield Corporation. There are two Westfield buildings in London - one called Westfield London that is located in Shepherd's Bush in West London, while Westfield Stratford City is located next to Queen Elizabeth Park in Stratford, East London.

Perhaps the main selling point of Westfield is the same selling point of most shopping centres: the convenience of shopping, dining, and even entertainment, all gathered together in one central location.

Both have extensive retail outlets, featuring a wide diversity of shops and stores and high street retailers from all over the world, Vue digital cinema, and a casino and luxury bowling alley in Westfield Stratford. You can pretty much buy anything within the shopping centre, whether you are looking for clothes, furniture, watches, cosmetics, jewelry, and many others.

Needless to say, places to dine in either Westfield are plentiful - Westfield Stratford has more than 70 places to eat, while Westfield London has a pleasant Southern Terrace where one can eat great food outside in good weather.

Chapter Four: A Feast For The Eyes

Now that you've settled in and eaten a hearty meal, you're probably wondering what's the next best thing to do. Confusion might dog the eager tourist at this point, because there are literally tons of things for the tourist to do and to see while on their London trip.

Try going easy at first - treat your eyes to some of the wonderful London museums before you begin to delve into this city's historical and cultural marvels. In this chapter, we present you with a literal Feast for the Eyes - some of the best and grandest museums in the world are located right in London, with unique exhibits and displays detailing the history of man, man's creativity, and man's ingenuity from all over the world. Watch the progress of British and London history - all within the walls of amazing and historical museum buildings that are free and open to all.

London has more than 200 museums - detailing British history and the history of the wider world, showcasing man's artistic creativity and ingenuity. From art to history to science and many others, taking a tour of London museums is an enriching and leisurely way to begin a trip around the capital.

1. *The British Museum*

The British Museum is located on Great Russell Street in Bloomsbury in London. It draws in about six million visitors each year - and no wonder: it comprises a collection of some eight million precious objects and artifacts, from many civilizations all over the world, spanning a period of more than two thousand years. Not only is it one of the largest museums in existence, it is also one of the most comprehensive in its documentation of human history and human culture from ancient times until the present. And best of all - it is absolutely free to visit.

The British Museum first opened in 1759 - the first national musuem in the world to be open to the public.

Though it began earlier - in 1753. It was largely based on the collections of physician and naturalist Sir Hans Sloane. Sloane was a collector, and he was able to accumulate around 71,000 objects such as books, prints, drawings, manuscripts, natural and historical specimens, and various antiquities from countries such as the Americas, Egypt, Greece, Rome, and the Sudan. He bequeathed this extensive collection "to King George II, for the nation, for the sum of £20,000."

An Act of Parliament formally established the British Museum, to which King George II gave his formal assent on 07 June, 1753. In addition to Sloane's collection, additional collections were added such as the Cottonian Library and the Harleian Library. In 1757, the Royal Library was added. These were the foundational collections of the first national museum that was fully open to the public, "belonging neither to church nor king, while aiming to collect everything." And it has remained true to this vision until today. Over the years, collections have been added from various sources, but the Museum still remains freely open to the public.

The Museum itself was originally housed in a converted 17th-century mansion - the Montagu House. The Museum's collection expanded, attracted a great number of people - until it because obvious that the Montagu House could no longer accommodate both its priceless contents as well as its numerous visitors. It was built upon successively over the years, and the grand neo-classical structure now features some unique highlights such as the Greek Revival style facade with 44 ionic columns topped by the sculptures by Sir Richard Westmacott called *The Progress of Civilisation;* the Round Reading Room; and the Queen Elizabeth II Great Court - the largest covered square in Europe.

A good tour of the British Museum would take about a day - and even then, you might still not be able to explore the entire museum completely. It is the largest museum in the world, with more than 100 galleries, not all of which are open to the public. It is estimated that approximately 50,000 items are available for public viewing, which is still only less than 1% of the museum's entire collection.

If you are planning on visiting the British Museum, it is a good idea to prepare beforehand and arm yourself with maps or floor plans - some of which are easily available online. This would enable you to easily find any specific display you are interested in. Or you can simply roam about and trust to luck, or join any of the free 20-minute spotlight tours provided by guides each Friday.

2. Tate Modern

Tate Modern is another one of London's most popular attractions - it is Britain's national gallery of international modern art.

Tate Modern is part of a quadruplet of art galleries - or the Tate Group, which comprises Tate Britain (also in London), Tate Liverpool, and Tate St. Ives.

Tate Modern is housed in the former Bankside Power Station that stands on the banks of the Thames. This power station is located directly across the river from St. Paul's Cathedral, its operation being shut down in 1981. It is a massive industrial brick building wtih a tall central chimney standing 99 m (325 ft) high, and features a gigantic turbine hall running along the center of the building, with the Boiler House in the north and the Switch House in the south.

The selection of this old building lent itself magnificently to the Tate's purposes. South of the Millenium Bridge, the revamped power station lends a creative industrial feel to its modern art collection - spanning a national collection of British art from 1900 to the present, as well as international modern and contemporary art.

Admission to the collection displays in Tate Modern is free, though they do occasionally hold temporary major exhibitions for which tickets must be purchased. There are free, guided highlight tours available daily. Works of Picasso, Dali, Bonnard, Cézanne, and Matisse are among the gallery's amazing collections.

Over the years, Tate Modern has expanded as the number of its collections, and its visitors, grew. Towards the south, there is a tower extension built over old oil storage tanks, which was converted into space for performance arts. The oil tanks themselves have already been converted usable spaces, and two of these tanks are occasionally used for live performance arts. The tower itself - the western part of the original Switch House, is ten storeys, or 65 meters high above ground level, and provides additional display and performance spaces, including facilities such as catering, parking, and retail space. There is a bridge that crosses the turbine hall to level 4 of the tower - which features natural top lighting.

Whether or not you are into modern art, there are famous historical works by renowned artists that are on display here, and which can be viewed for free. Sometimes shocking, sometimes breathtaking, there is an extensive collection of artworks in this gallery that are to be experienced as much as they are to be seen.

Tate Modern can be accessed via the south entrance, with Blackfriars being the closest station. It can also be reached from the north via the Millenium Bridge. A riverboat pier just outside the gallery offers commuter service, including Tate to Tate service - an easy riverboat commute from Tate Modern to its London counterpart Tate Britain.

3. *Tate Britain*

Tate Britain is touted as the "home of British art from 1500 to the present day." Throughout the years, it has also been variously called as the Tate Gallery, the Millbank Gallery, and the National Gallery of British Art (1897 to 1932). It is the oldest gallery in the Tate Group, and it is located on Millbank in London, having been built on the site of the former Millbank Prison.

Tate Britain used to house both British and modern collections, but with the establishment of Tate Modern, many of the more modern collections were moved to the new site. Historical and contemporary British art are still displayed in Tate Britain, which was consequently renamed because of this. Tate Britain holds works of artists such as William Hogarth, George Stubbs, Gainsborough and Reynolds, David Hockney, Peter Blake, Francis Bacon, and J.M.W. Turner, who bequeathed his entire collection to the nation.

As with many of the museums in London, admission to Tate Britain is free, although tickets may be purchased for major exhibitions. There are free, hourly tours available for sightseers, regular exhibitions, audio guides, interactive exhibits, lectures, and kids' activities. Each year, the Tate Britain also hosts the Turner Prize exhibition, a popular exhibition featuring four artists under the age of fifty.

This is a good second leg to a Tate viewing - a high speed boat ride can easily bring sightseers from Tate Modern to the Millbank Millenium Pier, which lies right outside Tate Britain.

4. National Gallery

The National Museum is currently located in Trafalgar Square, but it wasn't always. It used to be housed in Pall Mall, at the former house of insurance broker and patron of the arts John Julius Angerstein, after the British Government purchased his collection of 38 pictures in 1824 - which also comprised the original and founding collection of the National Gallery. In 1838, the collection moved to its current location in Trafalgar Square, Westminster in Central London, where its collection has expanded and grown until it now boasts the world's largest collection of Western European paintings.

The main building of the National Gallery - or the Wilkins building - eventually proved insufficient and inadequate for the purpose of housing a National Gallery - and it was added to, modernised, and expanded over the years. Only the façade which opens onto Trafalgar Square remains unchanged from the original design. One of the more recent extensions is the western Sainsbury Wing - a postmodernist addition built in 1991, and which now houses a collection of Renaissance paintings.

All the major traditions of Western European paintings are represented in the National Gallery, from late medieval, Renaissance Italy, and the French Impressionists. It now holds over 2,300 works, including works by famous artists such as Botticelli, da Vinci, Rembrandt, Van Gogh, Gainsborough, Turner, Renoir, and Gainsborough.

Admission to the museum, even for some special exhibitions is free, though tickets may be purchased for major loan exhibitions.

5. *National Portrait Gallery*

The National Portrait Gallery is the first of its kind, and is currently the largest collection of portraits and faces in the world.

Many consider the National Portrait Gallery to be one of the most appealing artistic and cultural displays in London, and it ranks highly as the most visited museums in Britain and in the world. Perhaps it is the sense of familiarity at seeing the history through the faces of many of the great British movers and shakers throughout the years - from kings and queens from the late 15th century, to artists and musicians, politicians, showbiz stars, explorers, authors, and media barons, to more modern personalities such as The

Beatles and JK Rowling. In this art gallery, it is more about the sitter or the subject than the artist, photographer, or sculptor.

Some of the notable portraits found in the National Portrait Gallery include the Hans Holbein cartoon of Henry VIII, the anamorphic portrait of Edward VI, Patrick Bronte's paintings of his sisters Charlotte, Emily, and Anne, a scupture of Queen Victoria and Prince Albert, and the famous but disputed portrait of William Shakespeare, also called the Chandos portrait.

The collection varies in selected mediums from photographs, caricatures, drawings, sculptures, paintings and self-portraits, grouped thematically and arranged chronologically. All together, there are nearly 11,000 works depicting notable and important British personalities featured in the National Portrait Gallery.

Admission to the gallery is free, and there are numerous changing exhibits of contemporary works, activities, and events such as the annual Portrait Prize competition. And to cap off your tour, there is a restaurant-bar-and-café at the top floor of the Ondaatje Wing that offers viewers a spectacular view of Trafalgar and Whitehall.

6. *Natural History Museum*

This is a perfect place to bring kids - and the kids at heart - where people can view a plethora of magnificent and awe-inspiring natural exhibits, all besides the magnificence of the building housing the museum itself.

The Natural History Museum, also sometimes called as the British Museum of Natural History, originated from the natural history collection of the British Museum, from which it was legally separated in 1963.

Sir Hans Sloane, the wealthy physician and naturalist, whose collection began the British Museum, was also an avid naturalist. When he left his collection to the nation after his death, much of it comprised the many different objects of natural history that he collected throughout his life - including dried plants, and human and animal skeletons.

None of Sloane's original natural history collections remain today - destroyed by the sheer failure of conservation by the natural history department of the British Museum. Then in 1856, newly appointed Superintendent of the natural history department Richard Owen led the British Museum's Natural History Department into the beginnings of what will later prove to be an exponential growth in depth and breadth.

Owen recognized the need for a bigger space for the natural history department, and this led to the purchase of land on Cromwell Road in South Kensington that would eventually be the site of the Natural History Museum. The building was designed in a Romanesque style that took about 7 years to complete. The construction made good use of terracotta tiles that would help preserve the museum's content from the climate and weather.

Originally, the plans included wings that would extend on both sides of the main building, but this was not continued due to budgetary reasons. Today, the space that should have been occupied by the two wings are the site of the Earth Galleries and the Darwin Centre.

London's Natural History Museum has grown to become both a museum and a research institute - specializing in the identification, classification and conservation of natural historical items and objects. Its permanent collection now number around 70 million objects, and some of the more popular objects include the skull of a Barbary Lion, a dodo skeleton, fragments of moon rock, a first edition of Darwin's "On the Origin of the Species," and the Wold Cottage meteorite - the oldest item in the museum's collection and which is thought to be around 4.6 billion years old.

Some of the exhibits that have proven very popular with kids are the Dinosaur gallery, with a horned Triceratops, a giant T-rex, and the fossilized skin of an Edmontosaurus; and a display of a blue whale and a giant squid. There are also interactive activities, exhibits, and trails that are perfect for adventurous children.

If that wasn't enough, the Museum's gardens also feature unique exhibits and displays, including a beautiful Wildlife Garden near the West Lawn, with a colony of honey bees.

Admission is, of course, free, though queues can sometimes be quite long. It is estimated that more than 5 million visitors come to the Natural History Museum each year, especially during school holidays.

7. *Victoria and Albert Museum*

The Victoria & Albert Museum, founded in 1852, and sometimes also referred to more simply as the V&A Museum, is dedicated to the preservation of more than 5,000 years of humanity's creativity in the field of decorative art and design.

The V&A is located in the Brompton District of the Royal Borough of Kensington and Chealsea, and houses a permanent collection of over 4.5 million objects. Its collection is eclectic, and includes virtually every medium of art since ancient times to the present day, from cultures all over the world. There are jewelry, silver, furniture, ceramics, ironworks, costumes, sculptures, prints, photographs, and a lot more, from the cultures of Asia, Europe, North America, and North Africa.

It is also the largest museum in the world. The physical site of the building covers an area of 12.5 acres (5.1 ha), and its 145 galleries span a distance of over seven miles. The building of the museum itself has been built upon over the years, and the predominantly Victorian style architecture of the grand and sprawling structure has been called a "palace for the people" - an ethos inscribed in the building itself.

Being for the people, admission to the V&A's permanent collection is free to the public, though there are fees for most of the temporary exhibitions.

It would be physically impossible to appreciate the V&A's entire collection in a single day - even if one could view the permanent collections within that time frame. For a tourist with limited time, it is recommended that you just wander and sort of take in whatever catches your fancy. There is also a café in the museum - the oldest in the world, and it is a chance to have British tea amidst splendid and beautiful surroundings. And don't forget to drop by the John Madejski Garden, especially at night, when the elliptical water feature and the planters are illuminated, as well as the surrounding façade of the museum building itself.

8. *Science Museum*

The Science Museum in London is located on Exhibition Road, South Kensington, where it is adjacent to the Natural History Museum. In fact, the two used to be connected by a public corridor, but this is now closed.

The building housing the Science Museum is known as the East Block, which was designed by Sir Richard Allison. It was intended to be a much larger construction project, but work stopped during the First World War, and was never continued.

The Science Museum came into being as an independent entity in June 1909, housing the Science

Collection that was kept separate from the Art Collection that can be found in the V&A Museum today. It is a popular attraction, and draws in about 3.3 million visitors annually. It is a perfect place to bring the kids - for whom the exhibits hold a natural appeal, making it a perfect family destination. There are seven floors of amazing, entertaining, educational and some interactive exhibits, including the Apollo 10 command module and a flight simulator, Stephenson's Rocket, and the Launch Pad where children are offered the first hand opportunity to experience basic scientific principles. The Space Gallery contains a 600 kg Spacelab x-ray telescope used for British space missions, and full-scale models of the Beagle 2 Mars Lander and the Huygens Titan probe.

For a fee, visitors can also visit the museum's IMAX 3D Cinema. The Dana Centre, on the other hand, where lectures and performances are given, is adults-only.

All together, the Science Museum holds a collection of over 300,000 items. They offer events such as "Science Night," where kids can spend an evening in science-based activities in the museum, and for a slightly older audience - outreach programs and educational trips.

9. *National Maritime Museum*

If you have children with you on your London trip, you simply cannot take a tour of London's museums without dropping by the National Maritime Museum. This museum features Britain's history with the sea, and together with the Royal Observatory, the 17th-century Queen's House, and Cutty Sark, was declared as a UNESCO World Heritage Site in 1997 - now referred to as the Maritime Greenwich World Heritage Site.

Britain has a rich maritime history, spanning commerce, naval interests, explorations, and travels, and the National Maritime Museum is a veritable treasure trove of more than two million items, including maps, art, memorabilia, artefacts, and various other precious objects commemorating hundreds of years of British exploration around the world. Greenwich was inevitably associated with navigation and the sea, and has been the home of the Greenwich Mean Time and the Prime Meridian since 1884. It is also home of the world's largest maritime historical reference library, named the Caird Library, that is open to all.

While the National Maritime Museum was first opened to the public in 1937 by King George VI, the building itself is much older - and originally served as a school for the children of seafarers, or the Royal Navy Asylum which was later incorporated into the Royal Hospital School.

Some of the notable exhibits are the sections that display James Cook's North-West Passage expedition in the late 1770's, the history of of the East India Company, the commemoration of the Glorious Revolution to the defeat of Napoleon, and the historic hero Admiral Lord Nelson and the Royal Navy. For families with kids, there is an interactive gallery designed for children with themed zones that include deck and ship models of a ship, a beach, and various other games.

10. Museum of London

If you want a good background into the City of London itself, the best place to go is the Museum of London. This is located on London Wall - a street that runs alongside remains of the original Roman-built London Wall, which is another important piece of the history of London. The Museum of London is part of the Barbican complex of buildings that have been redeveloped in a bomb-damaged area within the city.

It presents sightseers with a wonderful journey into London's past, from prehistoric times, through the Roman and Saxon periods, through medieval London, Victorian London, right up until modern times. The Museum contains around six million objects, and draws in more than one million visitors each year.

One of the best things about this Museum is that it was designed to be friendly to museum-novices and London history novices. There is only one route through the museum, and it is designed to take the sightseer chronologically through all the galleries, from prehistoric collections right up until the modern period.

There are artifacts from prehistoric London, displays and exhibits which take visitors through the city's years that included civil wars, plagues, and fires. In a very real way, it tells the story of the City of London, encapsulating the major events in London's history. There are interactive displays and exhibits, and it is open to visitors for free, with free daily tours available.

A leisurely jaunt through the Museum of London is also an enjoyable and leisurely way of orienting yourself to the City of London itself, and gives you a broader context as you begin to make your way through the rest of the city outside museum walls.

Chapter Five: Seeing the Past in London's Present

One of the most amazing things about London is how much of its long history can still be seen everywhere - coexisting along with its rich financial and cultural growth. It is a mishmash of many different historic structures from different periods located around each corner, all coexisting with more modern structures and buildings. It is a testament to over 2,000 years of the city's evolution, from the original Roman settlement of Londinium to today's modern skyscrapers.

Given how many interesting historic sights there are in London, it would be difficult not to have an involuntary historic tour just by walking down a street - almost all interesting sights in London come with a rich history and background. For that matter, it is also difficult to list all of the notable historic sights that tourists would be interested in. In this chapter, however, we try to present to you ten of the more popular historic sights that have drawn millions of visitors each year, notable for their roles in history, as well as a short background of each.

1. *Big Ben*

The name "Big Ben" is a bit of a misnomer - it is actually the nickname of the Great Bell inside the clock tower, which weighs more than 12 tons (13,760 kg). It strikes the hour, while four other bells inside the clock strike the quarter chimes. The tower itself is officially named Elizabeth Tower (formerly the Clock Tower or St. Stephen's Tower), but it is more popularly known today as "Big Ben," and is probably the most popular landmark in London today. It is the second largest four-faced chiming clock in the world - after Minneapolis City Hall.

Designed and built in the Gothic Revival style by noted architect and designer Augustus Pugin, it was part of an overall reconstruction for the Palace of Westminster after it was burned in a fire on October 1834. The entire project was led by chief architect Charles Barry, who relied heavily on Pugin's designs for the interior of the Palace of Westminster, and for the clock tower. The tower was Pugin's last design before he descended into madness and eventually, death.

Some of the interesting details of the clock tower include:

- The foundations of the tower are 10 ft concrete, founded on a 50 ft square raft, and is below ground level at 13 feet.
- The four clock dials are 180 ft above ground, and each is seven meters in diameter.
- The minute hands are 4.2 meters long, weighing about 100 kg (including the counterweights)
- The numbers on the clock are approximately 60 cm long
- The timekeeping is regulated by a stack of coins (pennies) which are placed on the huge pendulum
- There are Latin words under the clock face which translate to "O Lord, keep safe our Queen Victoria the First"

- A special light above the clock face is illuminated when parliament is in session

Construction of the tower was completed in 1859, and Big Ben's first ring was heard on July 1859. Prior to this, the first attempt at casting the massive bell failed when it cracked. The metal was melted down, and recast. A few months later, or on September of the same year, Big Ben also cracked. They rotated the bell and fitted a lighter hammer, and thus Big Ben has survived until today.

Although the origin of the name Big Ben is not known, there are two prevailing theories as to whom the bell was named after: Sir Benjamin Hall, the first commissioner of works, or Benjamin Caunt, a heavyweight boxing champion. Both men were sometimes affectionately called "Big Ben."

If you are not a UK resident, the bad news is that you cannot access the clock tower itself. Only UK residents are allowed a tour inside of the tower - and only after they have written and arranged it with their MP or a member of the House of Lords. There are no exceptions to this. And the waiting list is long - tours are often sold out up to 6 months in advance.

The most that one can probably do is to have a good view of Big Ben from vantage points such as the London Eye, the Shard, or the Monument.

2. *Palace of Westminster*

The best and closest you can probably get to a tour of Big Ben (from the outside) is by going on a tour of the Palace of Westminster.

Before it became the Houses of Parliament, the Palace of Westminster belonged to the crown as royal residences during the late medieval period, when it was known as Thorney Island. The earlier versions of the English Parliament met there, mainly because they followed the king. Later on, however, during the reign of Henry VIII, it was both a royal residence and used by the Houses of Parliament (where they had chambers) and the royal law courts - when it was called the Palace of Whitehall. It was added onto as Parliament clamored for more space within which it could conduct its day to day business.

In 1834, however, both Houses of Parliament were destroyed in a fire that originated from an overheated stove used to destroy tally sticks. While many of the buildings within the Westminster compound were saved, Parliament had no suitable place to meet. Temporarily, they met at the Painted Chamber and the White Chamber, both of which underwent hasty repairs.

King William IV tasked Parliament to make plans for its permanent accommodations, and each house created a committee for this purpose. The result was a competition for architects to submit proposals for the designated Gothic or Elizabethan designs - styles which Parliament pointed out as embodying more conservative ideals.

Charles Barry was granted the commission based on his Gothic-style plans, for a quadrangular building facing the Thames, and a tower in the center. Barry sought the assistance of Augustus Pugin, whom he tasked to design the Palace's interior, as well as the tower. In fact, it was likely because of Pugin's contributions that Barry was granted the commission.

The Palace of Westminster is built along a Perpendicular Gothic style, and features three main towers: the Victoria Tower, below which is the Sovereign's Entrance. At the north lies the Elizabeth Tower, more popularly known as Big Ben, and features the Great Clock of Westminster. And at the center of the building is the Central Tower - an octagonal tower, the shortest of the three, and rises above the middle of the building itself. There are turrets that line the top of the building, which have a more functional use of concealing ventilation shafts.

The oldest part of the building is Westminster Hall, which survived from the Palace's original designs. Altogether, the Palace of Westminster contains some 1,100 rooms, spread along 4 floors consisting of 4.8 kilometers of passageways.

Understandably, security is strict regarding visitors as there have been several assassination and bombing attempts and various other incidents throughout the years. There are always police on duty in and outside the building. Visitors may have access to the Stranger's Gallery in the House of Commons, but one has to pass through metal detectors and their possessions scanned. The Stranger's Gallery, or the Visitor's Gallery - is open to visitors who can view parliamentary sessions while they are in session. Lines are usually long, however, especially during popular debates, but UK residents may obtain tickets from their MP. One may also line up for a seat in a committee session, or visit the Parliamentary archives for research purposes.

When Parliament is in session, only UK residents may avail of the free guided tours inside the Palace, and only UK residents may apply for a tour of the Elizabeth Tower, or Big Ben. Overseas visitors, however, are allowed to partake of the tours of the Palace, but only during Parliament's summer recess.

It is one of the most visited tourist attractions in London, and has been classified - together with Westminster Abbey and St. Margaret's - as a World Heritage Site.

3. Westminster Abbey

Westminster's Abbey is a must-see for tourists. This beautiful, Anglo-French Gothic style church is not just the site of Prince WIlliam and Kate Middleton's royal wedding, it has also been the coronation church of the British monarchy since the 11th century. It is also the resting place of some of Britain's most famous people, including Dickens, Chaucer, Dr. Samuel Johnson, and Charles Darwin, as well as the grave of the Unknown Warrior - an unknown British soldier killed on the battlefield during the First World war.

More formally named the Collegiate Church of St. Peter at Westminster, Westminster Abbey is also part of the World Heritage Site that includes St. Margaret's and the Palace of Westminster. The Abbey's construction began in 1245, under the orders of King Henry III - who rebuilt it in honor of the royal saint Edward the Confessor, as well as intended the site for his burial. Prior to this, however, a church stood on the same site that was then called Thorn Ey, or Thorn Island. That church was intended to be a royal burial church by King Edward the Confessor. The first documented coronation here was that of William the Conqueror, and was since then the site of coronation of the Norman kings.

Currently, the abbey is classified as a "Royal Peculiar" - a collegiate church of the Church of England headed by a dean and responsible directly to the Sovereign, not to a diocesan bishop.

It was considered the third seat of learning in England, after Oxford and Cambridge until the 19th century, and it was here that the first third of the King James Bible Old Testament and the last half of the New Testament were translated. In the 20th century, it was here that the New English Bible was put together. They say that if you look closely, you can see schoolboy graffiti from the 1700s to the 1800s littering the walls.

The abbey is open to the public regardless of religious denomination, and anyone is free to attend any of the worship celebrations: Morning Prayer, Evensong, and the Eucharist. The abbey has been known to be actively involved in worship and song, and many of Britain's famous musicians, singers and composers are linked to the Abbey, though the choir singers of today are the Choir of Westminster Abbey, no longer the monks from the tenth century.

Attending one of the services is a good way to gain entrance to the Abbey for free, but there are also guided audio tours with individual entry tickets - these tours are available in other languages such as German, French, Spanish, Italian, Russian, Portuguese, Mandarin Chinese, Japanese, and Hungarian. Tickets cost around £20.00 for adults, and £9.00 for children.

4. *Tower of London*

Located on the north bank of the Thames River, the historic Tower of London is both famous and infamous. The central point of the Tower of London was the White Tower, built by William the Conqueror in 1078, after the Norman conquest of England. It was both a keep and a military strongpoint, likely an effort of William the Conqueror to secure his hold on the conquered land, as the Normans replaced the old Anglo-Saxon ruling class. He wanted to over-awe the restless and resentful population, and he set about an extensive castle-building scheme all over conquered England.

The White Tower was meant to protect London, to represent power and status, it served as a gateway to the capital, while also serving as a royal residence. It is one of the largest and most preserved 11th-century fortresses in Europe.

The White Tower was built along the lines of Norman military architecture, but the layers of sprawling construction that one recognizes now as the Tower of London was the result of structural additions by succeeding kings. An inner "ward" was built by Richard the Lionheart during his reign, and later on, an outer ward around the castle was built by Edward I. Edward I also built a Tower Wharf along the bank of the Thames, which was later expanded by Richard II. Altogether, the castle covers an area of around 12 acres (4.9 ha), and a further 6 acres (2.4 ha) surrounding the castle was cleared land for military reasons - referred to now as the Tower Liberties.

In the next 1,000 years, the history of the British monarchy played itself out within the walls of the Tower of London - much of these events shaping England's history in the struggle for the crown. It served as royal residences, a prison, defensible fortifications, a symbol of oppression, the site of murder and torture, a menagerie, mint, and an armory and barracks. It was also the repository for the Royal Wardrobe, as it houses the crown Jewels since the 17th century until this day, where they are on public display. The stories told of the Tower of London are magnificent, eerie, disturbing, but always compelling - stories of intrigue, murder, ghosts, and even myths, such as the Tower Ravens upon whose comings and goings the monarchy's fortunes depended - and which birds are, to this day, under the care of the Yeomen Warders. It is valued as much for the historical events that have transpired within as for its sheer historical value.

These days, it is both a museum and a popular tourist destination, and was declared a UNESCO World Heritage Site in 1988.

5. Tower Bridge

If things had turned out differently, London's Tower Bridge might now look completely different. When commerce began to pick up in London sometime in the late

1890s, it was decided that another crossing over the River Thames was needed - but because the River Thames was an active London port area, ships and boats also sailed actively up and down the river. Somehow, the need for crossing over the river needed to be reconciled with the right of way of passing ships. Prior to this, the shortest way of crossing the river from Tower Hill to Southwark was through the Tower Subway - which was eventually closed in 1898 after most pedestrians began using the Tower Bridge. Today, the Tower Subway is now used for water mains.

More than 50 designs were submitted, and it was a design by Sir Horace Jones that was eventually approved. His design involved a bascule bridge with two bridge towers and a central span that split into two equal bascules, both of which would be raised to allow river traffic passage. Above it rose an open air pedestrian walkway accessible via stairways. But soon after construction began, Jones died and George Stevenson took over. The original brick facade design by Jones was replaced by a more ornate Victorian Gothic Style, which Stevenson felt would harmonize the bridge with the nearby gothic style Tower of London.

Construction began in 1887, and took all of eight years to complete. It involved two massive piers, containing over 70,000 tons of concrete, that were sunk into the riverbed. 11,000 tons of steel were used for the framework of the towers and walkways, which were then clad in Cornish granite and Portland stone.

The bridge was officially opened on June 30, 18944. It connected the Iron Gate on the north bank of the river with Horselydown Lane on the sought - at present, these are known as the Tower Bridge Approach and the Tower Bridge Road, respectively.

Critics were not very receptive to the bridge in the beginning - calling it tawdry, pretentious, and absurd. In 1910, the high level walkways were closed because it became the haunt of prostitutes and pickpockets. It was reopened only in 1982, this time with an admission fee.

These days, the tower footbridges - which were replaced by glass walkways in 2014, are very popular among tourists. Rules of signaling control the passage of river traffic through and across the bridge, and coloured lights are used at night. Two red lights means that the bridge is closed, two green lights mean that it is closed. If it is foggy weather, the sound of a gong was also used. Ships or vessels passing through are required to display signals or blasts from their steam whistle, and there the suspension of a black ball from the walkway indicated that the bridge could not be opened.

Tower Bridge is still fully functional today, and it is estimated that around 40,000 people cross every day. It has been renovated in 2008-2012, prior to the 2012 London Olympics, and now there is a mandated 20 mph speed limit and 18 ton weight limit for crossing vehicles. Ship crossing still takes precedence, but some 24 hours' notice is required before the bridge can be opened - which are published in advance. The bascules are raised on the average of about 1,000 times each year.

Tickets can be purchased to gain admission to the Tower Bridge Exhibition - which details the history and mechanism of the bridge, and is housed in the twin towers, the high-level walkways, and the Victorian engine rooms. There are films, photos and interactive displays for the benefit of the sightseer.

6. *Churchill War Rooms*

Anyone with an interest in World War II and Nazi Germany's defeat would certainly be interested in the room in which Churchill and his wartime government had its headquarters and command center. This secret bunker in the heart of London was where they they coordinated their plans and strategies throughout the second world war.

Located beneath Westminster, the Churchill War Rooms - formerly called the Cabinet War Rooms, and now more formally referred to as the Churchill Museum and Cabinet War Rooms - is now preserved as a museum and is part of the five Imperial War Museums. The rooms are preserved now as they once were in 1945.

These rooms were built and completed about a week before war broke out - a foresight of the Royal Air Force who anticipated the aerial bombing of London. The plan was for the dispersal of key government offices to the suburbs and elsewhere in the country, but to have a suitable temporary emergency site for a government center in London. This was identified as the basement of the then New Public Offices, on the corner of Horse Guards Road and Great George Street, near Parliament Square - now the Treasury Building in the Whitehall area of Westminster.

These rooms became operational shortly before war broke out in Europe - by which time they accommodated the civilian government or the Cabinet, who coordinated closely with senior military forces in the Central War Room. Then a few days later, Poland was invaded and Britain declared war on Germany. Some of the other features of the bunker included a Map Room and a Cabinet Room. When Churchill was appointed Prime Minister, he visited the Cabinet Room and decided: "This is the room from which I will direct the war."

After the Blitz bombing of 1940, protection of the Cabinet War Rooms was increased by "the Slab" - a massive layer of concrete that was up to five feet thick. The rooms continued to expand, and now included facilities and dormitories for the staff, private bedrooms for officers and senior ministers, and rooms for telephone swithchboard operators and typists. Two of the more prominent rooms include the Transatlantic Telephone Room and Churchill's office-bedroom.

These rooms were abandoned shortly after the surrender of Japan in 1945, and the preservation and administration of this historic site was tasked to the Imperial War Museum in the early 1980s. They were subsequently opened to the public in 1984. It was expanded in 2003, restored, and rebranded as the Churchill Museum and Cabinet War rooms in 2005. One of the centerpoints of the museum is an interactive centerpiece table that allows visitors to access digitized material from the Churchill Archives Center. The Museum is estimated to receive around 300,000 visitors each year.

7. St.Paul's Cathedral

St. Paul's Cathedral caters to the Anglican denomination, and is the mother church of the Diocese of London and the mother church of the worldwide Anglican Communion. It is one of the most recognizable landmarks in London, and sits on Ludgate Hill at the highest point in the city of London.

The cathedral was designed and built by Sir Christopher Wren in the English baroque style, but this constructed only after the fire of 1666 destroyed the previous St. Paul's cathedral. Actually, four other churches were built on this site, and each time the cathedral was expanded and extended. Wren was originally tasked to renovate the old church, but the Great Fire completely destroyed the old church, including 89 other churches in London. In 1669, three years after the fire, Wren was designated to design and constructed a new church. Construction began in 1675, and was completed in 1711.

One of the more prominent features of St. Paul's Cathedral is the large dome - long been a notable sight of the London skyline. Until 1967, the cathedral was the tallest building in the world, and to this day, its dome is still among the highest in the world.

St. Paul's Cathedral is at the center for many significant national events, such as the funerals of Lord Nelson, the Duke of Wellington, Sir Winston Churchill, George Mallory, and that of Margaret Thatcher, as well as services which marked the end of the First and Second World Wars. It was here that the celebrated wedding of Prince Charles and Lady Diana Spencer took place, and where thanksgiving services were held for the Diamond Jubilee of Elizabeth II.

There are eight arches which support the dome, which weighs about 66,000 tons and reaches a feight of 111 meters (366 ft). There is a large lantern at the top of the dome that weighs 850 tons. Visitors can reach the top of the dome via three galleries: The Whispering Gallery, and Stone Gallery, and the Narrow Golden Gallery. The latter encircles the lanter's base, and gives one a magnificent view of the city of London.

Beneath the cathedral is the largest crypt in Europe, built under the entire building. This was designed to contain the massive piers which were designed to provide structural support to the building whose weight is spread out over eight piers. The crypt is also the final resting place of some of Britain's notable personages such as the Duke of Wellington, Admiral Nelson, and even Christopher Wren himself, who designed and constructed the cathedral.

Admittance to the cathedral is only free for services, and there is no sightseeing during this time. There is a charge for sightseers, for which The Interpretation Project has been formulated - a long term project dedicated with breathing life into St. Paul's for its visitors. There is a film that tells the history and the daily life of the cathedral, and multimedia guides were launched in 2010. These guides offer close up views of the interior artwork of the ceilings, galleries, and the dome, including mosaics, paintings, and photographies. Paid-for-admission, which costs around £18.00, but are also offered at group and student rates, also includes entry to the Cathedral floor, the crypt, and the three galleries in the dome.

8. *Hampton Court Palace*

Aside from his many wives, the famous and infamous King Henry VIII was also known for his extravagance - which included many palatial residences. Two of these survive today, and of the two (the other being St. James's Place, which is still in use by the royal family), the Hampton Court Palace was known to be his favorite residence.

Hampton Court Palace is located in Richmond, upon the Thames in Greater London. It was originally a property of the Order of St. John of Jerusalem, before it was taken over by Thomas Wolsey, the Archbishop of York, after Henry VIII's Dissolution of the Monasteries. Wolsey was the

Chief Minister and a favorite of Henry VIII, but after he fell from the king's favor, he passed the palace on to the king as a gift. He died soon after.

The king took over the palace, and began to expand it. While Henry VIII had over sixty houses and palaces, few were large enough to accommodate the entire king's court. Part of the renovation included the large kitchens, which were quadrupled in size, the Great Hall, and the Royal Tennis Court. Prior to this, Wolsey had spent extravagantly for the palace, and much of his renovations still remain today. There are state apartments for the king, a courtyard called the Base Court, and forty-four lodgings for guests, and his renovations were a harmonious blending of Rennaisance, perpendicular Gothic, and Tudor styles. This was largely due to the effort of Italian craftsmen who specialised in adding Renaissance ornamentations to Tudor construction.

The palace was actively used by the succeeding Tudor monarchs, until King Charles was executed in 1625. Hampton Court passed to the Commonwealth, now presided over by Oliver Cromwell, and much of the contents were auctioned off. After the Restoration, it was restored to the crown, and subsequently renovated by the succeeding monarchy, which included the addition of rich tapestries and paintings.

The Great Hall was mainly retained, however. Some of the other notable features of the palace include the Great Vine Vineyard, the famous Court Maze, and 60 acres of formal gardens. There is a replica of the crown of Henry VIII on display, a Chapel Royal, the King's Beasts, the magnificent state rooms of the king, and of course, the vast kitchens.

And because it was the scene where much of the Tudor monarchy drama has been enacted, there are also stories that abound regarding the place. In fact, the House s itself is probably as compelling as the stories of the kings and queens who resided there.

It is believed that the last king to reside in the palace was King George II. It was opened to the public in 1796. Today, paid admission includes audio guides, costumed tours, and daily talks and programs.

9. *Guildhall Art Gallery and the Underground London Roman Amphiteatre*

The Guildhall Art Gallery was constructed in 1999, replacing a building that was destroyed in The Blitz in 1941. It was intented to house the art collection of the London. It was built in a semi-gothic style, adjacent to and in harmony with the nearby historic Guildhall, to which it was connected internally. Within the art gallery, sightseers can witness an amazing display of some of the masterpieces of great artists, which are dated from 1670 to the 21st century. A different kind of display, however, can be seen underground.

Beneath the Guildhall Complex lies the remains of an old Roman Amphitheatre. It was discovered in 1988, when the old Guildhall Art Gallery was being redeveloped. Today, the remains of the ampitheatre are displayed on site in the basement of the art gallery.

The Romans established the first major settlement along the River Thames during AD43, which they called Londinium. It was suspected for a long time that the Romans had built an amphitheatre in old Londinium, but it wasn't until the remains were found that this theory was validated and the site determined. It was previously thought that the amphiteatre was built outside of London's city limits.

Much of the ruins are still remarkably well-preserved. It was a circular, 80-m structure that would have accommodated around 6,000 people. During that time, Londinium's population would have been around 20,000-30,000. Today, many of the amphiteatre's original structure remains - and one can see portions of the original circular walls, its drainage system, and even the sand that filled the arena. In it heyday, it featured gladiator combats, public executions, wild animal fights, and even religious activities. When the ancient Romans left, the amphiteatre was abandoned, and lost for centuries until recently.

There are various ways by which a sightseer can join a tour of the old amphiteatre - admission to the Guildhall Art Gallery includes entry to the amphiteatre, but there are also tours conducted by other bodies such as the Museum of London, although general admission is free. Booking a tour is highly recommended, however, as this would enable the spectator to learn more and gain some experience from lectures or reconstructions conducted by the guides.

Aboveground, a wide circular design on the stones of Guildhall yard marks the outline of the amphitheatre below.

10. Cutty Sark

The Cutty Sark was legendary - the fastest clipper of her time, now remarkably well-preserved and on display in Greenwich, London, where it is now an award-winning attraction.

The ship was built in a Scottish shipyard in 1869, commissioned by a shipping magnate named Jock "Whitehat" Willis. It was considered a masterpiece, its design of timber and iron was both sleek and strong, and with three masts that were capable of holding a spread of canvas that could drive the ship to a speed of up to 17 knots. She proved herself on the high seas when she sailed as one of the tea clippers of Britain, and became known as one of the fastest ships afloat.

In fact, she was often involved in one of the many tea races during her time - tea was fashionable, and since the first batch of the new tea harvest from China was much coveted and fetched a high price, an annual tea race became a sensation, with one of the more famous races that between the Cutty Sark and the ship Thermopylae. News was reported in the newspapers and the telegraph, and people placed bets on the outcome. Though Cutty Sark never did make it to the finish line, she was undoubtedly considered one of the fastest ships, often referred to as a "speck on the horizon."

But the Cutty Sark's popularity soon degenerated. When the Suez Canal was opened, steamships with larger cargo capacities now had a faster route to the Far East, and tea clippers like and sailing ships were no longer in demand. The Cutty Sark was no longer in use in the tea trade. Her captain, Tiftaft, died in Shanghai, and was replaced by the first mate, James Wallace. She was now commissioned to carry various cargo all around the world, including coal, castor oil, jute, and tea to Australia.

In 1880, while on her way to Japan to deliver coal for the American Pacific fleet, a fight broke out on board the Cutty Sark. One man was killed. Captain Wallace, however, allowed the man responsible to leave the ship, which resulted in a mutiny among his men. As the situation degenerated, Wallace committed suicide by jumping overboard. He was replaced by William Bruce, who was, however, a drunk and notoriously incompetent. He set sail without inadequate provisions, and the crew starved. After an inquiry in New York in 1882, Bruce was suspended and replaced by Captain Moore. By this time, Cutty Sark's reputation had become that of a cursed vessel.

Her owner, Jock Willis appointed as captain Richard Woodget, who decided to turn Cutty Sark for use in the wool trade to Australia, and. Once again, Cutty Sark outdid herself, and her record speed continued to improve.

Once again, steamships proved tough competition, and by this time, the Cutty Sark was already past her heyday. She was sold to a Portuguese company, who renamed her Ferreira. For the next 25 years, she carried various cargo to and from Portugal, Africa and the

Americas. In the 1920s, she was purchased by Captain Dowman, who brought her back to Britain where she was essentially restored and opened to the public under her original name, Cutty Sark. After Dowman's death, Cutty Sark was used by cadets for training drills by the Navy Training College of Greenhithe. She set sail for the last time in 1938, crewed by cadets on a journey from Falmouth to the Thames.

Facing the scrapyard, Cutty Sark was rescued by the Cutty Sark Preservation Society - led by the Duke of Edinburgh. She was hoisted up onto a dry dock in Greenwich, where she is now on display to commemorate Britain's maritime history and heritage, and serve as a memorial to the Merchant Navy. She is preserved as a museum ship, and part of the National Historic Fleet. She is a prominent landmark in Greenwich, London.

Visitor can immerse themselves in the ship's environment, experiencing the life of her former Victorian seamen - taking the helm, enjoying a view of the River Thames, or walk underneath her to touch her original hull planks and iron framework.

Chapter Six: Out And About In London

One of the best ways to tour a place is by walking, and this is certainly true of London - where something surprising always lies at the next corner.

From parks to cemeteries to more modern tourist attractions, this chapter brings together some of London's sights that are best seen on foot. So strap on your walking shoes, and explore London while you're out and about!

1. *The London Eye*

This is a magnificent engineering and architectural structure that stands in the Jubilee Gardens on the South Bank of the River Thames, next to Westminster Bridge. Simply put, it is a giant ferris wheel - 443 feet (135 m) tall, with a wheel diameter of 394 feet (120 m), and was the world's tallest ferris wheel in 1999, before it was eventually surpassed by the the Star of Nanchang, the Singapore Flyer, and the High Roller in Las Vegas.

It is still considered the tallest Ferris Wheel in Europe, and is also called "the world's tallest cantilevered observation wheel" - a reference to the single side supporting A-frame, as opposed to those in Nanchang and Singapore, which are supported by frames on both sides.

More often referred to as "the Eye," "the London Eye," or less popularly but more accurately, "the Millenium Wheel," this giant and futuristic-looking Ferris wheel was designed by the husband and wife architectural team of David Marks and Julia Barfield - who had the idea of a large observation wheel - which they presented in a competition for a landmark design commemorating the new millenium. While there were no winners in that competition, their persistence - and the backing and the sponsorship of the British Airways - eventually saw the construction and completion of the iconic Eye.

Its construction was done in sections - each section floated up the Thames on barges, and assembled on flat, piled platforms. Once fully assembled, it was lifted upright in two phases, the second phase taking place after the interval of a week. The rim of the Eye is supported by tensioned steel cables, and is connected to the spindle by eighty wheel spokes.

The London Eye traded hands a few times since it was first opened to the public in March of 2000. Depending on who owned it and their prevailing sponsorship and branding contracts, its name also changed - thus, it had also been called by various names such as British Airways London Eye, the Merlin Entertainments London Eye, the EDF Energy London Eye, and more recently, the Coca-Cola London Eye - whose sponsorship contract started on January 2015 and would last for about two years.

Resembling a huge spoked bicycle wheel, the Eye took about a year and a half to complete, and used more than 1,700 tons of steel and more than 3,000 tons of concrete for the foundation and the structure itself. It features 32 sealed and air-conditioned ovoidal passenger capsules, each of which weighs 10 tons, and is able to hold up to 25 people. Seating is provided inside these capsules, although people are free to walk around inside. These capsures are attached to the wheel's external circumference, and allows sightseers a magnificent view of London as the wheel rotates.

The London Eye does not usually stop to take on passengers - it revolves at a very slow speed of about 0.9 kph or 0.6 mph - moving a distance of 26 cm (10 in) per second - so passengers could easily get on or off at ground level even while the wheel is in motion. A complete revolution takes about 30 minutes. It is stopped, however, when disabled or elderly passengers embark or disembark, to afford greater safety to its passengers.

This isn't precisely a traditional Ferris Wheel as it is more an Observation Wheel - thus, it is as much about the ride as it is about the sights. Each passenger capsule allows sightseers a magnificent 360 degree view from a height of 443 feet (135 m) - and clearly visible are some of the famous landmarks of London such as the Buckingham Palace, St. Paul's Cathedral, Big Ben, Westminster Palace, the Tower of London, the Tower Bridge, Westminster Abbey, and the Houses of Parliament. On a clear day, one can see for a distance of around forty kilometers (25 miles). The view can be exceedingly breathtaking at night, when the city of London lights up.

Be aware that the queues for a ride on the London Eye can be very long - and this applies for the lines to purchase tickets and those for embarking on the passenger capsules. You might want to book your tickets early unless you plan on spending hours waiting in lines. During the longest evenings of summer, rides are open until 9:30 in the evening.

As of June 2008, it was estimated that around 30 million people had ridden the London Eye since it first opened in March 2000.

2. Hyde Park

If you'd rather stretch your legs in the wide outdoors, neither will London disappoint. There are eight royal parks in London, each connected to the other, the largest of which is Hyde Park, which is located in Westminster.

King Henry VIII confiscated Hyde Park from the monks of Westminster Abbey, and enclosed it as a private hunting ground. Later on, it was opened to the public by King Charles I in 1637. Kensington Palace lies on the far side of Hyde Park, and William III constructed The King's Private Road - a gravel carriage track that still exists today, though it is now more commonly known as Rotten Row.

Hyde Park covers an area of more than 360 acres (142 ha), and its landscaped terrain boasts several popular sights and attractions including the large artificial lake called the Serpentine, Rotten Row which is now mainly used for horse riding and jogging, and the Speaker's Corner which was a popular meeting place where people were allowed to speak their political or religious views during the riots of 1872.

Later on during the park's history, Decimus Burton was commissioned to bring Hyde Park within the ambit of Buckingham Palace, and for this he laid out a series of paths, driveways, lodges, and a large gate called the Grand Entrance or the Apsley Gate to transition between the park and the palace. This arch, later called the Marble Arch, was later moved to a different location, and culd now be seen near the Speaker's Corner.

The park also featurs a memorial to Princess Diana, a Holocaust Memorial, and a fine selection of various statues, sculptures scattered across the grounds, including that of the Drinking Horse, the Vroom Vroom, Genghis Khan, Still Water, Achilles, and the Joy of Life Fountain, among others.

Hyde Park is mainly open grassy areas dotted with large trees, but there is an exceptional rose garden located in the southeast corner.

A visitor can simplywalk around enjoying the scenery or the marvelous sculpturs and structures in the park, and for a refreshing break, there are two lakeside restaurants which can offer anything from a simple refreshment to a full course meal. Or, one can engage in one of many recreational activities inside the park such as swimming, boating, cycling, tennis, and horse riding. There are regular open air events such as concerts in the park, and some of London's orators can usually be seen at Speaker's Corner on Sundays, expounding expressively on their diverse views and opinions.

3. *St. James Park*

London has eight Royal Parks, the oldest of which is St. James's Park. St. James's Park's name was derived from James the Less, to whom it was dedicated.

The park covers an area of 57 acres (23 ha) in the city of Wesminster, right in the center of London. It was originally a marshland area through which the Tyburn stream flowed. It was bought by Henry VIII in 1532, but it wasn't until 1603, under James I, that the area was drained and landscaped. It became a kind of menagerie housing exotic animals such as camels, crocodiles, an elephant who was supposedly given more than four liters of wine every day, and several exotic birds in aviaries.

It was redesigned again by Charles II, based on the influence of France from the time that he spent in exile in that country. The king used the newly landscaped area to entertain his guests, and it was also opened to the public. During this time, however, the park was notorious for being a meeting place for acts of lechery.

Later on during the 17th and 18th century, part of the canal was reclaimed, and Buckingham House was purchased. Subsequent redesign and works included the conversion of the canal into a lake, rerouting of the pathways through the park, and the Marble Arch was built at th same time that Buckingham House was redesigned and expanded into Buckingham Palace. The park was opened to the public in 1887. By this time, the Marble Arch was moved to its current location at the junction of Oxford Street and Park Lane.

Some of the prominent features of St. James's Park include The Mall - the site of many ceremonial parades and national event celebrations; various water birds including the much-celebrated white Pelicans at the lake; Duck Island; The Blue Bridge; The Tiffany Fountain; and the Horse Guards Parade.

This is a relaxing ocean of green in the heart of the city of London, where people can stroll by the lake, enjoy the lush flower beds, watch the ducks, or relax in a deck chair. The park draws in millions of visitors and tourists each year.

4. *Kensington Gardens*

Kensington Gardens was once the private garden of Kensington Palace. It covers an area of 270 acres (111 ha), and lies between the City of Westminster and the Royal Borough of Kensington and Chealsea.

It is separated from the neighboring Hyde Park (from which it was believed it had been taken), by the West Carriage Drive and the Serpentine Bridge, which forms the boundary between the two parks. Kensington Gardens is more formal than Hyde Park though, and is only open to the public during daylight hours.

The western area of Hyde Park was taken and separated as Kensington Gardens at teh request of Queen Caroline, who had it professionally designed as a landscaped garden. It was also during this time that the Serpentine was created, by the damming of the eastern outflow of the River Westbourne. The part of the Serpentine that lies within Kensington Gardens is referred to as "The Long Water."

Some of the famous featurs of Kensington Gardens include the Round Pond, a sunken Dutch garden, the Italian Garden, the Albert Memorial, the Serpentine Gallery, Speke's monument, and Elfin Oak. There are magnificent flower beds, various statues and sculptures, and two playgrounds one of which is the popular Diana, Princess of Wales Memorial Playground. There is also a Peter Pan statue in the park, in honor of the book "Peter Pan in Kensington Gardens" by J.M. Barrie, which is a prelude to Peter's Neverland adventures.

People can enjoy a stroll amidst formal avenues of magnificenet trees and lush flower beds, or enjoy some refreshments at the Broadwalk Café, which is open daily.

5. *Trafalgar Square*

It can be argued that Trafalgar Square is the center of London activity. People gather here for various events such as rallies, marches, Christmas celebrations, and even open-air cinemas. It is surrounded by many important buildings such as the National Gallery and St. Martin-in-the-Fields. Nelson's Column, in honor of Britain's greatest military hero, rises magnificently from the center of the square, dominating the area from its 52 m height. The square was named Trafalgar in commemoration of the Battle of Trafalgar of 1805, when the British Royal Navy routed the combined forces of France and Spain. Admiral Lord Nelson died in action, however, and became a celebrated British hero.

The square was designed in the 1820s and built in the 1830s by architect John Nash, but it had been neglected for several years, taken over by traffic, and flocks of feral pigeons. It was only in 2000 that the square was transformed into the Nash's original design: traffic was banished, the pigeons were shooed away, and a pedestrian plaza was built.

There are four huge lions at the base of Nelson's column, and four plinths at the four corners of the square. There are also currently two fountains that commemorate David Beatty and John Rushworth Jellicoe, admirals of the Royal Navy, though these were added later, in 1939.

The square has now become a multicultural center, and some of the best free music and dance events are held here during the summer. It is also the center of London's bus network, and of Night Bus trips.

Some of the interesting facts about Trafalgar Square include the Nazi's plan during the war to bring Nelson's Column to Berlin to signify a successful invasion. Norway also denotes a magnificent Christmas tree to the square every year as a thank you to Britain for its liberation from the Nazis.

6. *Kew Gardens, or the Royal Botanic Gardens*

The Kew Gardens has been classified as a UNESCO World Heritage Sight - and some call it the world's most famous garden.

Also referred to as the Royal Botanical Gardens, the Kew Gardens serve as an international botanical research and education institute. It has one of the most diverse collection of plants in the world, with over 30,000 kinds of living plants and over seven million preserved plant specimens. It is one of London's top tourist attractions.

There is certainly plenty to see. Kew covers an area of 300 acres (121 ha), and the beautiful landscape features several ornamental gardens, a soaring treetop walkway, tropical glasshouses, various other plant houses, ornamental buildings, cafés, galleries and museums, and the smallest of the royal residences - Kew Palace.

The site is over 250 years old, and began as a private farm known as Kew field. The exotic garden at Kew Park was actually a private one, begun by one Lord Capel John of Tewkesbury. It was subsequently enlarged and developed, and became the Kew Gardens after the merging of the royal estates of Richmond and Kew in 1772. Much later, or in 1840, it was adopted as a national botanical garden. Its area was expanded considerably by the Royal Horticultural Society. Today, it is under the active management of the Royal Botanic Gardens, Kew, under the protection of its own police force, the Kew Constabulary, which has been in operation since 1847.

Each of the different glasshouses have a maintained temperature or climate that can reach up to 27°C, and inside these magnificent glass buildings are numerous amazing exotic plants and trees. One can literally walk in a seemingly endless exotic adventure through the gardens, with discoveries at every turn. One needs only to pay admission to the gardens, after which admission to the galleries and the museum is free.

7. *Highgate Cemetery*

Highgate Cemetery is located in north London, on both sides of Swain's Lane in Highgate, next to Waterlow Park, and is included in the Historic England Register of Parks and Gardens of Special Historic Interest in England.

Highgate Cemetery opened in 1839, in an effort to provide seven, large and modern cemeteries outside central London. Most of the cemeteries in London then were attached to churches, and they had long since been unable to accommodate the steadily accummulating number of burials in London.

The original design of Highgate Cemetery was created by architect Stephen Geary. Eventually, this became a fashionable burial place, and Gothic tombs and buildings soon dotted the area. The area was expanded, and it is now divided into the East and West Cemetery, and is a working cemetery to this day. It is also considered a nature reserve.

It is estimated that approximately 170,000 people are buried in Highgate, including some notable personages such as Douglas Adams, George Eliot, Michael Faraday, Karl Marx and a variety of other Socialist leaders and thinkers, and many others.

Aside from the gravesites of famous and notable people, Highgate Cemetery is an amazing labyrinth of Victorian structures such as chapels and catacombs, and Gothic tombs and buildings. Two areas in particular - the Lebanon Circle and the Egyptian Avenue, are considered of outstanding architectural importance. The cemetery combines natural, cultural and historic elements to create a solemn, picturesque resting place for the dear and departed. It is an eerie but compelling place, and it has long captured people's imaginations - featured in film and literature as the setting of various ghost, occult, vampire, or other paranormal stories. In fact, from the 1960s to the late 1980s, it was featured in popular culture as the haunt of the "Highgate Vampire."

The East Cemetery can be viewed daily, though guided tours are available - usually only on the first Saturday of each month. The overgrown West Cemetery can only be viewed by a guided tour - this is due to incidences of vandalism and souvenir hunters looting some of the displays. Both East and West Cemeteries charge a fee to enter. Take note that there are also restrictions on taking photographs inside the cemetery.

8. Sea Life London Aquarium

The Sea Life London Aquarium was first opened in March 1997, first being known as the London Aquarium. It is located on the ground floor of County Hall, at the South Bank of the River Thames, near the London Eye.

In 2008, the aquarium was purchased by Merlin Entertainments, and underwent a £5 million renovation and refurbishment, including a new underwater tunnel, Shark Walk, and a renovated Pacific Ocean Tank. When it was reopened in 2009, it was called the Sea Life Centre. In May 2011, a penguin exhibit was also added.

The Sea Life London Aquarium affords sightseers with an amazing view of marine life through its many glass aquariums and interactive exhibits and displays. It houses thousands of sea creatures, the most popular exhibit being the Shark Reef.

Currently, the aquarium is also actively involved in marine conservation efforts, awareness campaigns, marine management and preservation, and even in breeding programs of marine life such as Cuban crocodiles, seahorses, butterfly goodeids, and jellyfish.

The aquarium welcomes about a million visitors each year. Tickets are charged for admission, and one can go on a tour of the aquarium for additional costs.

9. *Millennium Bridge*

A relatively recent addition to London's sights, the Millennium Bridge is a steel suspension bridge that stretches over the Thames River for a total of 325 meters (1,066 ft), and a 4 m wide deck for pedestrian traffic. It can hod up to five thousand pedestrians at any given time, and links St. Paul's Cathedral to the north, and to the south is near the Shakespeare's Globe and the Tate Modern Museum. It was the first major bridge crossing the Thames that was built the Tower Bridge in 1894, and the first bridge dedicated exclusively to pedestrian crossing.

In preparation for the celebration of the new millenium, the Southwark Council sponsored a competition for the design of the new Millenium Footbridge. The winning entry was "the blade of light" by Arup, Foster and

Partners, and Sir Anthony Caro. It was designed with supporting cables below the deck level, so as to preserve the view of the landmarks in the surrounding areas - Globe Theater, Tate Modern, St. Paul's Cathedral, the Tower Bridge, and the Shard. The view is exceptionally breathtaking at night. Today, it is a tourist attraction and London landmark in its own right.

The bridge did suffer from some problems in the beginning. It was finished two months behind schedule, and barely a few days after opening, people noticed a certain infirmity in its structure. It was thereafter named "The Wobbly Bridge" or "The Wibbly-Wobbly Bridge." To address these vibrations that were noticed by the passing pedestrians, the bridge was closed and underwent modifications - and it remain closed until February 2002, two years after the New Millenium. It did seem to work, however, for no significant wobbling has been noticed in the bridge since then. It is always open to the public, except for maintenance or in very high winds.

10. Piccadilly Circus

Piccadilly Circus is essentially a public square located at the junction of five main roads: Regent Street, Shaftesbury Avenue, Piccadilly Street, Covent Street, and Haymarket. It is a wildly recognized modern landmark - and the illuminated billboards have made it a popular picture the world over. And because it is surrounded by several major tourist attractions such as the Criterion Theater, London Pavilion, and Shaftesbury Memorial - including being at the heart of numerous restaurants, bars, clubs, shopping and other entertainment destinations, and even an underground tube station - it has since become a busy area where people congregate and mingle. This chaos of activity has led to the expression, "Busy like a Piccadilly Circus."

Its unique name derives from Piccadilly Hall, a house which belonged to a tailor famous for selling piccadills (different kinds of collars), while "Circus" derives from Latin which means "circle" - a reference to being a round, open space at a street junction.

At the southeast side of the Circus stands the Shaftesbury Memorial Fountain - formerly located in the middle of the square prior to the end of World War II. It features the Greek god Anteros, an "angel of Christian charity," though is nowadays more commonly mistaken for Eros, who was actually his brother.

These days, it is generally overcrowded and always busy, so it might not appeal to the tourist who desires a quiet place to enjoy London's sights. The fact that it is teeming with life, however, may appeal to some - and it is a wonderful place to sit and watch passing people, take photographs, or simply as a place to congregate and meet up prior to exploring the many tourist spots or surrounding commercial establishments. One can easily walk towards Soho, Chinatown, Leicester Square, and Trafalgar Square from the Piccadilly Circus. It is certainly a great way to orient yourself during your London sightseeing tour.

There are certain notable features of the Piccadilly Square which the sightseer might find interesting: the bright Coca Cola sign has been on display in Piccadilly Square ince

1955, though the lights were switched off on two occasions - the funerals of Winston Churchill in 1965, and that of Princess Diana in 1997. On the west side of the circus, there sits an old Police public call box - dating from 1935, and one of the very few of its kind that survives to this day. And finally, the seven noses of Soho are also reputed to be located in the circus, and it is said that anyone who finds all seven will have great wealth.

Chapter Seven: Interacting With London

London isn't just a city filled with magnificent architecture, landscaped parks, historical sites, and glorious collections of artworks - it is also teeming with life and culture.

Don't spend all your time in London visiting museums and watching the sights. Immerse yourself in the rich and colorful cultural life of London - whether ancient, cultural, artistic, or downright macabre!

1. *Buckingham Palace and the Changing of the Guards*

Buckingham Palace is the London residence and administrative headquarters of the reigning monarch of the United Kingdom. It is the center of many state banquets, court ceremonies, and other national events and celebrations. One can usually tell if the queen is in residence because of the hoisted flag.

Because the royal family still does occupy the palace, the building itself is generally not open to the public, although tours are conducted for visitors during the summer months - when the Royal Family is not in residence. Such tours usually include the viewing of the Changing of the Guard - a ceremonial event which draws many tourists each year. Even if you have not chosen to join a tour of the palace, you can still get to watch the Changing of the Guards for free, which are held in front of Buckingham Palace at around 11:30 in the morning, and lasts for about 45 minutes. From April to July, the Changing of the Guards is held daily, while they take place on alternate days from August to March. Because this event is very popular, visitors are usually advised to arrive early to get the best view. Sometimes though, this ceremony may be canceled due to weather conditions.

The Changing of the Guards is a traditional ceremony wherein The New Guard arrives from Wellington Barracks and takes over the responsibilities of the Old Guard. The guards are garbed in their traditional red tunics and bearskin hats. This is done in a formal ceremony that is accompanied by music, presenting of arms, and a formal handing over of the Palace keys.

2. *The Royal Mews*

The Royal Mews has been deemed the finest working stables in the world. It is located in Buckingham Palace, and houses Britain's royal collection of historic coaches and carriages, carriage horses, and the state vehicles and motor cars. Perhaps the finest - certainly the most dazzling of the entire collection is the famous Gold State Coach - which was used in the Golden Jubilee celebrations in 2002.

The name originates from the first royal stables in Charing Cross, which housed the royal hawks, back in 1377. The hawks were confined in the stables during moulting ("mew") time, hence the name. After it was destroyed by a fire in 1534, it was rebuilt as a stable, though it kept its former name. It was redesigned by William Kent in 1732, and was opened to the public in the 19th century.

The Royal Mews is responsible for all road travel undertaken by the Royal Family. It was moved to the grounds of Buckingham Palace in the 1760s. The old mews in Charing Cross was demolished, and Trafalgar Square was constructed on the old site. The current stables/garage called the Royal Mews was designed and constructed by John Nash in 1825, though there have been extensive modifications since then. To this day, it remains open to the public throughout much of the year.

3. London Dungeon

The original London Dungeon started in 1974, on Tooley Street, and was initially intended to be museum of macabre history. It was not, strictly speaking, a dungeon, but its original location was once used as a "pillory" to punish thieves, or to imprison arrested drunks.

In 2013, however, after nearly 39 years, the attraction was moved to its present location near County Hall and the London Eye, where it draws a great number of tourists each year.

The attraction isn't for the faint of heart – costumed actors, special effects, riveting props, and unique shows and rides lead the sightseer through an unforgettable journey of horror, excitement, and the macabre. In fact, one of its advertisement posters was once banned for being "too scary."

But perhaps what makes the London Dungeon so compelling and iconic is that many of its displays and shows are based on facts – what one might consider the darker side of the history of London. Truth, as they say, is stranger than fiction. Legends are also heavily drawn upon to complete the atmospheric effect.

Some of their more iconic shows feature Henry VIII, Bloody Mary of Tudor fame, Sweeney Todd, and of course, Jack the Ripper. There are also shows that focus on the darker moments of more than 1,000 years of London's history, and includes such events as the Bubonic Plague of 1665, and the Great Fire of 1666.

The attraction is owned by Merlin Entertainments, who also own The London Eye. A walkthrough through the place would take about 90 minutes, during which the visitor should expect the unexpected, and be ready for a pretty realistic journey through London's murky past.

The London Dungeons has also been referred to as the "museum of horrible history." Granted one does not really expect to see actual historical objects that are well-preserved, but it certainly preserves the stories and legends from London's darker side.

4. Open Air Cinemas

In recent years, Open Air Cinemas have been steadily growing in popularity in London - particularly during the summer months. These film showing events have become like festivals, most often than not located in stunning locations or environments, and some even offer gourmet food and cocktails. From rooftops to old manor houses, to some of London's magnificent parks, those large screens are popping up everywhere, and people are coming to watch. The experience of a wonderful surrounding, snugly wrapped in a blanket, and watching some of your favorite movies - is an experience that is difficult to beat.

You are going to have to do your research to find the next venue, and their date and time of showing. The good news is that there is a wide variety to choose from, and you can take your pick based on location or the movie currently showing. Some of the more popular Open Air Cinemas now operating in London include:

- Nomad Cinema
- Luna Cinema
- Rooftop Film Club
- Film4 Summer Screen
- Backyard Cinema
- Summer Nights Film Festival
- Cult Screens
- Floating Cinema
- St. Kat's Floating Film Festival
- Pop Up Screens

5. *Regent's Park Open Air Theatre*

If theater is more your thing - certainly a more unique way of experiencing London - then you must check out Regent's Park Open Air Theatre.

This theatre has been a feature of Regent's Park since 1932 - founded by Sydney Carroll and Robert Atkins, and it is leased by The New Shakespeare Company Ltd - a registered charity - from The Royal Parks. Shows are usually scheduled from May to September. Just beware that there may be cancellations due to the weather, in which case the theatre allows for exchange of tickets under their Weather Policy.

The open theatre is located within Queen Mary's Gardens, in the Inner Circle of Regent's Park, right in the middle of the park. The theater is completely uncovered, save for the area underneath the auditorium - and the theater has an extensive backstage that is fully equipped to put on some of the best and classical stage performances and adaptations. From comedy, drama, musicals, and a regular dose of Shakespeare, all performed in the midst of lush trees and wonderful scenery, it is a wonderful way to experience a bit more of London's theater scene.

6. *Madame Tussauds*

Madame Tussaud is Marie Tussaud, born Marie Grosholtz in 1761, in Strasbourg, France. Her mother worked for Dr. Philippe Curtius of Switzerland, a physician skilled in wax modeling. Dr. Curtius was the one who taught Marie the art of wax modelling.

Marie made wax sculptures of many famous people, and even made death masks of some prominent victims during the French Revolution. These death masks were used as revolutionary flags, and paraded through the streets of Paris. When Dr. Curtius died, she inherited his vast collection of wax models, and now married, she travelled around Europe showing her collection.

After the Napoleonic wars, she was no longer able to return to France. She settled down in some of the upper rooms of Baker Street Bazaar in Great Britain, and then later opened her museum of wax figures in London. She died in 1850, though some of her original wax creations exist to this day.

Because of the increasing need for more space, in 1883, her grandson Joseph Randall transferred the museum to its current locatin on Marylebone Road. This was formally opened in 1884, and were a great success. Eventually, Tussauds was sold to a group of businessmen because of disagreements within the family shareholders.

Today, Madame Tussauds is a major tourist attraction in London, and in the entire world. It is currently owned by Merlin Entertainments, who acquired it rom the Tussauds Group. They have since opened branches in other locations in the world, such as Berlin, China, Singapore, Thailand, Australia, North America, and in various other locations in the United Kingdom and in the United States.

Perhaps the great popularity of Madame Tussauds is how a visit within its walls brings you face to face with some of the more prominent persons in world history - from celebrities, politicians, artists, writers, and even murderers - some of those who have moved prominently in the world are preserved in amazing, lifelike poses that make you feel as though you are literally face to face with the real person. So lifelike are the wax figures, in fact, that a statue of Adolf Hitler has often been the target of much disapproval - there was a significant clamor for the removal of Hitler's statue from the London museum, while Hitler's wax head was ripped off from its statue in the Berlin branch.

Madame Tussaud's unique and ingenious displays of her creative wax sculpting has long been recognized, and even celebrated in popular media - warranting mention in books, films, and these days, even computer games. Don't forego the chance to marvel at her unique artistic vision in the original city in which Madama Tussauds began - right in the heart of London.

7. *London City Farms*

Here is an alternative to enjoying the great outdoors within the city limits - as opposed to spending an afternoon in grand estates and parks, one can visit some of the city farms that have been been steadily growing in popularity among tourists and visitors.

This is a wonderful way to mingle with the life and bustle of a working farm, all within the concrete jungle of London. There are cute and sprightly animals, all furry and cuddly and scaly types. A visitor also has the option of riding horses, having a picnic, milking cows, partaking of farm fresh meals, feeding animals, and just enjoying the simplicity and joy of a countryside farm within London.

If this appeals to you, you have several options among the well-known city farms, including:

- Hackney City Farm
- Vauxhall City Farm
- Spitalfields City Farm
- Kentish Town City Farm
- Mudchute Park and Farm
- Deen City Farm
- Hounslow Urban Farm
- Surrey Docks Farm
- Stepney City Farm
- Brooks Farm

Visiting any of these farms is a wonderful way to spend time with your family in London - particularly if you have kids; and a good way of imbibing farm fresh products. These farms usually offer visitors various activities and events to involve them in farm life, and a great way of bonding with the London community.

8. 221B Baker Street

Literary aficionados and fans of Arthur Conan Doyle's iconic detective genius Sherlock Holmes should not pass up the opportunity to drop by Baker Street - where Sherlock had his apartment, and which street now features the Sherlock Holmes Museum.

One interesting fact about the street is that when the Sherlock Holmes stories were written, Baker Street addresses did not reach as high as 221B. When the street was finally extended in 1932, the Abbey National Building Society moved into 219-229, and thereafter had to hire a fulltime secretary just to answer Sherlock's mail. Later on, the Sherlock Holmes Museum was opened just a few doors down, and there ensued between the two premises a 15-year dispute as to who had the right to receive 221B's mail. Abbey House closed in 2005, however, and since then, the Museum's right to the address has not been challenged.

The Sherlock Holmes Museum, on the other hand, opened in 1990, and though technically it is not at 221B (it lies between numbers 237 and 241), it was allowed to bear the number 221B by permission of the City of Westminster.

The Sherlock Holmes Museum is a private museum housed in a Georgian town house that is dedicated to the famous detective and his fictional exploits. Relive some of Sherlock's more famous and infamous moments through some of the displays and exhibits in the museum.

And if that isn't enough, you can make your way to Northumberland Street near the Charing Cross railway station, where stands the Sherlock Holmes Pub. It was opened in 1957, when its owners, Whitbread & Co., were able to own the entire Sherlock Holmes exhibit by the Marylebone Borough Library and the Abbey National. The pub was remodeled to a late Victorian form, and in its interior, the exhibit includes a detailed replica of Holmes' fictional apartment.

9. *London Pubs*

Within the metropolis of Greater London, it is estimated that there are over 7,000 pubs where a person can get a pint. It would certainly be difficult to wean out the best out of all the many good pubs currently operating, and so a visiting tourists has many options to choose from.

Telling stories and sharing a pint within a public house is another unique English experience - one which has existed for a very long time - some would say since before Shakespeare's time.

While each of the thousands of London pubs would certainly have its own merits to recommend itself, visitors may derive unique experience from trying out some of the traditional and historical pubs which have been in business for a very long time. Here are a few choice selections to choose from:

- The Nag's Head, near Harrods and Knightsbridge
- The French House, Soho for a more French style pub
- The Dog and Duck, Soho, reputed to be the watering hole of George Orwell
- The Lamb and Flag in Covent Garden, said to be the area's most historic watering hole, and catered to such names as John Dryden and even Dickens
- The Lamb is a beautiful, well maintained Victorian style pub, again boasting of having served Dickens
- Ye Olde Cheshire Cheese is often a favorite tourist destination and offers a unique atmospheric treat, as well as stories of some literary giants who have sat within its walls - yes, Dickens included
- The George Inn is a truly historical pub - it is the only pub in London owned by the National trust, and is the last remaining galleried inn in London. The place was even mentioned in Dickens' Litter Dorrit as a coffee house the author once visited.

10. The View From the Shard

The Shard is a 96-storey skyscraper in Southwark, London. it is 309.6 metres (1,016 ft) high, is the tallest building in theUK, the fourth tallest building in Europe, and the 105th tallest building in the world. Can you imagine what the view will be like from the top?

You don't have to wonder - you can go and see it for yourself, as there is a privately operated observation deck, also called The View from the Shard, which was opened to the public in 2013.

The building was designed by Renzo Piano, pursuant to a planned redevelopment of Southward Towers. The UK government encouraged the developmen of tall buildings at major transport hubs, and in 2003, the plans were approved.

Construction began in February 2009, and the building was completed in 2012.

Piano envisioned the building as a "spire-like structure emerging from the River Thames." Interestingly, its name derives from a criticism of the building, as the English Heritage claimed that it would be a "shard of glass through the heart of historic London." Since then, it has been commonly referred to as "The Shard."

The View from the Shard is a tourist attraction, and is located on two viewing platforms inside the Shard - the first a triple level indoor gallery on level 69, the second a partially outdoor gallery on level 72. This is complemented by a gift shop on the ground floor, and "The Sky Boutique" on level 68 - dubbed "the highest shop in London."

The View from the Shard was opened to the public on February 2013. To date, it is one of the most popular attractions in London, and the Shard has already become an international London landmark.

Tickets are all pre-booked, timed and dated, though a few tickets are available for purchase on the day.

Chapter Eight: The London Night Scene

London becomes more vibrant at night - and where there are people who don't sleep, there are places where they can go. London boasts massive and diverse nightspots that you should definitely check out. Not sure where to start? Here's a few ideas to get you started!

1. *The Ceremony of the Keys*

The Ceremony of the Keys is an ancient custom where the gates of the Tower of London are formally locked. This has been carried out every night for the last 600 years, since it was first begun in 1340. It is akin to a routine of locking up all the doors at night - but carried out in a more formal ceremony, given the location, the implied trust of the king or queen, and not to mention to presence of the Crown Jewels inside the tower!

The ceremony begins at precisely 7 minutes to 10 o'clock. The Chief Yeoman Warder of the Tower emerges from the Byward Tower, carrying a candle lantern and the Queen's Keys.

He moves to Traitor's Gate, and hands the lantern to an escort. The party then moves to the outer gate. After he locks the outer gate, The Chief Yeoman Warder and his escort retrace their steps, locking the Middle and Byward Towers as they pass. They then return to Traitor's Gate, where another sentry awaits.

"Halt! Who comes there?"

"The Keys!"

"Whose Keys?"

"Queen Elizabeth's Keys."

"Pass Queen Elizabeth's Keys and all's well."

They proceed through the archway and up the steps where the main guard is drawn up. The order is given to the Guard and the Escort to present arms. The Chief Yeoman Warder raises his bonnet high and calls "God preserve Queen Elizabeth." The guards answer: "Amen" - at precisely the same time, the clock chimes ten, and the Last Post is sounded. The keys are taken to the Queen's House, and the guards are dismissed.

Tickets for admission to watch this ceremony is free, but it is advisable to book them in advance - which you can only do online, where there is a £1 transaction charge.

They admit as many as 40-50 people each night, and they can be very particular about do's and don'ts - for instance, they don't admit latecomers (visitors are escorted inside at precisely 9:30), and you should be able to present an ID to confirm your identity as the ticket holder. Taking photographs and mobile phones are not allowed during the ceremony, and neither are there any toilets or refreshments available. The ceremony itself is short - so it behooves the visitor to behave while it is taking place. Afterwards, visitors are again escorted outside at around 10:05 pm.

2. *West End Theatre Productions*

If someone told you to "see a West End show" during your trip to London, you might wonder where the "West End theatre is." There is actually no such thing. The reference actually refers to different theaters located in a common area - sometimes identified informally as Theatreland - located in the West End of London.

London - the birthplace of William Shakespeare - has a rich theatrical culture. There are over forty venues in Theatreland, and there are a number of other theatres nearby - despite not being located in the West End, they are still considered part of Theatreland - which is, after all, more a reference to the theatrical culture than to specific geographic locations. Many of these are privately owned theatres, and the theatre buildings are usually of magnificent architecture - grand neo-classical, Romanesque, or Victorian bulidings, with fabulous interiors and decoration. West End theatres cater to a large number of tourists and spectators each year - an estimated 14.5 million tickets were sold in 2013 alone.

Productions vary from musicals, classics, modern straight plays, and comedy performances. There are also long-running shows such as *Les Misérables, Cats,* and *The Phantom of the Opera.* By far, the longest-running production in the world is *The Mousetrap* - a non-musical play by Agatha Christie, and has been performed continuously since 1952.

Check out the list of running shows, and if there is one that catches your fancy, book your tickets as soon as possible! You might also want to explore theatres outside of West End London - this often gives you a choice of greater variety in both the shows and the location. There are some small theatres, or theatres located above pubs - that also offer performances to interested audiences.

3. *Shakespeare's Globe*

Are you hankering instead for some Shakespeare? Check out Shakespeare's Globe - a modern reconstruction of the original playhouse that was built in this area in 1599, then rebuilt again in 1614 after it was destroyed by fire, before it was demolished again in 1644. It is located on the south bank of the River Thames, in Southwark, and is more formally known as "Shakesperare's Globe Theater."

The construction of Shakespeare's Globe is largely due to the efforts of American actor and director Sam Wanamaker. The location is not precisely the same as the original building - due to the riverside concerns, and the building itself has had to be adjusted for modern safety issues. All in all, it is as close a reconstruction of the Globe Theatre during Shakespeare's time. The completion of this project (which took more than 20 years) also sparked the founding of several Shakespeare's Globe Centres all over the world.

The theatre opened in 1997, and has been putting on regular plays since then. Performances are usually scheduled for the summer, between May and the first week of October. There is also a Sam Wanamaker Playhouse within the site - a smaller, indoor playhouse in honor of the man whose vision was responsible for the reconstruction of Shakespeare's Globe.

If you still haven't had enough Shakespeare - there is also an Exhibition regarding Shakespeare's life and works. Why not start out with a tour of the two theatres - which are offered regularly - and learn about the history of the site, the original theatres, their destruction and reconstruction - including the Rose Theatre, Globe's neighboring theatre and competitor. Then settle in to watch a play. Including Shakespeare's plays, of course, they also put on performances of plays that were written by Shakespeare's contemporaries - from 1576 to 1642.

4. *Hyde Park's Bat Walking Tour*

There are actually a number of places in London where one can see bats in flight - particularly during summer evenings. They can usually be seen near ponds, lakes, rivers, canals, sheltered glades, and wooded areas. Hyde Park, however, offers an interesting alternative - a Bat Walking Tour in Kensington Gardens and Hyde Park at night.

Not only is it a chance to see the magnificent Kensington Gardens and Hyde Park - but you get to do so at night (which presents its own attractions), in the company of a expert guide.

Those who attend are given a short lecture on how bats hunt, what are bat facts and myth, and what are the different species of bats. To add to your expectations of the evening - other nocturnal animals may also make an appearance - perhaps an owl or the occasional fox.

This is a great tour for children and adults, and a chance for children to be out at night in the company of their parents. Book your tickets via the Royal Parks website - where you can also see the Bat Walk schedules.

5. Hampstead Observatory - see the night sky

If you want to look farther up than the flight of bats in the sky, and right into space, you can't beat a visit to Hampstead Observatory - the only free observatory in London.

The observatory is located in a cul-de-sac near Whitestone Pond in Hampstead. It was founded by the

Hampstead Scientific Society in 1899, and dedicated it to the bringing of scientific enlightenment to everyday Victorians. It has been a steady draw for villagers or visitors - especially on nights of the full moon or any other spectacle in the heavens. On regular days, some 10 to 50 people share the telescope, but expecct as many as 100 to 500 visitors if there is a major event going on above.

The observatory features a 6-inch Cooke refracting telescope from 1898 that is mounted on a concrete pier underneath the opening of the domed roof. This is an equatorial telescope, which means that as the earth revolves underneath your feet, the stars also move quickly across and out of your view. You can track the movement of stars, and since the whole roof opens, you have complete access to the sky.

As an alternative, there is also a smaller, portable telescope available, and visitors are also welcome to bring their own telescopes.

Beside the observatory is a weather station which has been recording meteorological readings continuously since 1910 - the longest record in London.

The Hampstead Observatory is open to the public from mid-September to mid-March, from 8-10pm Fridays and Saturdays, and 11 am to 1pm on Sundays - only on clear nights. To cap off (or perhaps begin) your visit, you might want to attend one of the regular lectures of the Society at St. John's chuch hall.

6. *London Comedy Bars*

If you want a break from the solemnity and seriousness of the first four options, or if the weather simply won't allow you to go wandering around in London, you can try and visit one of London's many comedy clubs and treat yourself to a few good laughs.

There really is a wide variety to choose from, for instance:

- Always Be Comedy (ABC) at Kennington, Putney and Brixton
- Up the Creek in Greenwich
- Camden Comedy Club, in the upstairs room at 100 Camden High Street
- 99 Club Leicester Square at the Storm Nightclub in Leicester Square
- Amused Moose Piccadilly at Piccadilly Square
- Shambles at the basement of Aces & Eights
- Angel Comedy at N1's Camden Head pub
- The Comedy Grotto
- Old Rope at The Phoenix in Cavendish Square
- Banana Cabaret at The Bedford in Bedford Hill
- Piccadilly Comedy Club at the Comedy Pub
- Laugh Out Loud London - with about several branches in London, including Camden, Islington, Victoria Park, Stoke Newington, and Brixton
- The Comedy Store at Oxendon Street, near Piccadilly Circus

7. London Live Music

What could be better than a clear, balmy night and good music with its strains reaching to the heavens, thundering over the ground, and pulsing through your body? You might not be able to play your stereo at full volume at home, so you might as well get out of the house and listen to the thundering strains of live music. The live music tradition is strong and healthy in London, and you have a wide range of options to choose from.

Depending on the type of music you like - opera, rock, jazz, or punk, with world-famous artists or new talent putting on regular performances, there's a lot to choose from for the music aficionado.

Here's a few venues you can explore - look at their schedules and lineups, and settle yourself down to an enjoyable evening!

- Union Chapel in Islington is perfect for intimate concerts
- Enjoy the high ceiling, wide rooms, and great atmosphere of the Roundhouse
- For something a bit more classical (or sometimes not), check our Barbican Hall
- Cecil Sharp House, popularly dubbed as the most prestigious venue for folk acts and acoustic music
- Jazz strains beautifully at Ronnie Scott's, a premier Soho jazz club
- If rock is more your thing, try the Brixton Academy
- The Tabernacle on Notting Hill caters more to grassroots artists, though they do boast a history of great stars such as The Rolling Stones and Pink Floyd
- For a younger crowd, explore The Barfly, at Chalk Farm Road - this is where Coldplay, Muse and The Killers once played
- An amazing venue can be found at Bush Hall, at Shepherd's Bush, and is a great spot to appreciate acoustic music

Don't limit yourself, though. London's selection of live music performances go far beyond this short list. Explore. Enjoy.

8. *London Pub Crawl*

Would you like to make the rounds of some of the best pubs in London but don't know where to go or how to start? Or are you worried about maybe drinking too much, paying too much, or simply how to get around London pubs at night while staying safe and still having a good time?

Try going on a pub crawl. These are organized tours (so to speak) of the different pubs in London, conducted by locals who knows all that you need to know about having a fun night out. They know the hottest spots, will watch out for you until the night ends, and best of all - because these are usually organized in groups - they bring together many fellow travelers for a great night out in London.

Check out London Gone Wild, Camden Pub Crawl, London Party Pub Crawl, among others. Just remember to exercise due discretion in which pub crawl you sign up for, who you are with, and what you do (or don't do). And of course, be sure that you are of legal drinking age - which is 18 years in the UK. And remember also that smoking has been banned in all indoor public places in the UK, including pubs - though some do offer a smoking area patio.

9. *London Nightclubs*

The London night scene does not discriminate - if your type of music is the one you can dance to - in a friendly crowd with a similar penchant for getting loose on the dance floor, London also has a wide variety of nightclubs for the aficionado.

Want to know more? Here's a list of some of London's popular nightclubs to get you started:

- The Drop in Stoke Newington
- Paramount Bar is located on the 31st floor of Centre Point at New Oxford Street
- The Loft is located above The Old Shoreditch Railway, on Kingsland Road
- For some cutting edge electronic music, try out Fabric on Charterhouse Street
- Corsica Studios at Elephant Road
- Cable, located underneath London Bridge Station
- The Nest, a basement club in Dalston
- Love & Liquor, a celebrity haunt that is also pretty pricey, but with great music, located at Maida Vale
- The Old Queen's Head, a local favorite, on Essex Road

10. London By Night Tours

Ever wanted to see London's landmarks and tourist spots at night? Now you can - guided night tours offer visitors a new perspective on London - a different, somehow more haunting and exciting place after the sun comes down.

Check out your old favorites: Big Ben, The Houses of Parliament, Westminster Abbey, St. Paul's Cathedral, the Tower of London, Tower Bridge, the London Eye, Piccadilly, and a lot more.

These tours have proven exceptionally popular among tourists, and is definitely a must-see for everyone.

There are different types of tours available - by bus (recommended for families), by foot, by boat, and even by bike. These tours are led by informative and entertaining guides - some haunting and frightening, some awe-inspiring and breath-taking, and some simply marvelous. London almost becomes a different, perhaps more vibrant city when the sun goes down and houses and buildings are lit up - or sometimes, when the only illumination is from candles, the moon, or the stars.

Chapter Nine: Off London's Beaten Path

London draws millions of tourists each year, and the various tours, walks, and exhibits being offered to its visitors is a thriving industry.

Sometimes, though, a person may hanker for something that is different and unique - something that is perhaps not so grand, and maybe something that is downright sinister.

It would be difficult to encapsulate or even list the myriad attractions in London - history is there at every corner. The good news is that there is also no shortage of hidden gems, and secret spots or tours that - even if they may not be completely secret, they are at least less crowded compared to London's major tourists attractions.

This chapter contains ten of London's less well-known attractions, less mainstream haunts - and an offer of a different perspective to the historic grandeur that one usually sees on a typical London visit.

1. *St. Pancras Old Church*

While nobody could pinpoint the precise date at which St. Pancras Old Church existed, it seems certain that it is one of the oldest sites of Christian worship in England - likely as old as St. Pancras himself. St. Pancras was a Roman martyr who was beheaded sometime in 304 AD, and it is claimed that St. Pancras Old Church has been in existence since the 4th century, "a site of prayer and meditation since 314 AD."

There is some speculation that the location was a site of worship even before St. Pancras church - that of Roman pagan worship, before pagan temples were converted to Christian use in the 7th century by early missionaries .

Roman tiles and other Roman features were certainly found in the church's foundations and in its vicinity, but other than that, there is no reliable evidence to bolster the claim of a pagan worship site that is generally located at a crossroads - what is known as a Roman *compitum*.

St. Pancras Old Church is located in Somers Town in central London, and should not be confused with the St. Pancras New Church, which is located on Euston Road. Though historically, they did serve the same congregation - St. Pancras Old Church was abandond by the surrounding population in the 14th century - probably because of flooding concerns and the existence of better wells at Kentish Town. When the New Church was consecrated, services were held in the old church only once a month. Eventually, the Old Church fell into disrepair. For a time, it became a haven for Catholics - as it was then an isolated and unused church. According to some, the last bell which sounded mass in England was that in St. Pancras. It was one of only two churches in England (the other was Paddington Church) where Catholics were allowed to be buried.

By the 19th century, population had grown south of the old parish, and it was decided to restore the old church. This was undertaken by Alexander Dick Gough - and he expanded and enlarged the church, while also reworking its exterior. During its reconstruction, it was noted that the walls contained several Normal materials such as columns, pilaster piers, and other remains - leaving them to conclude that the old church might originally have been a Norman structure.

The remodeling and repairs did save the church from ruin, but had the unfortunate consequence of destroying the ancient and historical interest of the old church.

The church's interior still does provide some clues to its history - old memorials, grave slabs, and even alcoves where statues and other religious decorations may have been placed.

St. Pancras Old Church is not precisely a tourist destination, but this unassuming church saw a lot of history. And despite its restoration, its foundations still threatens its longevity as there are already cracks in the wall that might be caused by the ancient drains underneath it.

One of the more notable features of St. Pancras Church is its churchyard - which is discussed in the section below.

2. Hardy Tree

Perhaps one of the first things you might notice about the St. Pancras Old Church cemetery is how high its ground level is. People ascribe this to how a burial ground is constantly used and reused - and the ground level rises as more soil is added on top of the old graves.

There are a number of notable people buried in this churchyard, including miniaturist Samuel Cooper (Cowper), and Johann Christian Bach, among others. One notable feature is a mausoleum designed by architect John Soane for himself and his wife - a Grade I listed tomb that inspired the design for England's iconic red telephone boxes.

Interesting trivia also surrounds this cemetery. It was mentioned in Dickens' "A Tale of Two Cities" as a location of body snatching which were used for dissection in medical schools. It was also the place where Percy Bysshe Shelley and the future Mary Shelley planned their elopement - when they met at the grave of Mary Wollstonecraft, Mary's mother. But perhaps the most striking feature of this cemetery is that which is known as "the Hardy Tree."

Sometime in the 1860s, during the time of the great railway expansion, lines were being built to serve the Midland Railway's stations at King's Cross and St. Pancras. But when the proposed route crossed a graveyard, Thomas Hardy (Tess of D'ubervilles, Far from the Madding Crowd, The Mayor of Casterbridge, and Jude the Obscure) - then an apprentice architect, was tasked to relocate the old cemetery.

The young Hardy relocated the graves, and a cluster of hundreds of overlapping gravestones found its new home in a tight ring around an ash tree in the St. Pancras cemetery grounds. Some think that it was this distasteful task which inspired Hardy's poem "The Levelled Churchyard."

In June 1877, the old churchyard was reopened as St. Pancras Gardens.

3. Hyde Park Pet Cemetery

This old pet cemetery isn't precisely being kept a secret - but it isn't actively being promoted either. For those in the know, however, it can be an interesting and eye-opening visit.

Somewhere amidst the bushes of Victoria Gate Lodge's Garden and behind the gates of the perimeter of Hyde Park, is a plot of ground littered with miniature headstones celebrating the life and death of some of Victoria London's beloved pets.

It was started in 1881, when the old lodge keeper, Mr. Winbridge, agreed to bury a Maltese Terrier named Cherry in his backyard - by the request of her grieving family who had made friends with the lodge keeper and had spent many enjoyable times in the Park. Cherry was laid to rest in a splendid ceremony, and her grave is marked by a tombstone with the inscription "Poor Cherry. Died April 28, 1881."

The idea caught on, and soon the site became the place of internment of many of London's dead and deceased but not forgotten pets. Mr. Winbridge became a sort of unofficial caretaker of the tiny cemetery, which was pleasantly laid out in neat rows of tiny tombstones bearing loving epitaphs. It can be an amazing journey for anyone - not only because of the raw emotions that are conveyed in some of those inscriptions, but also seeing death in miniaturized form - preserved from an era that was generally known for its prudishness and restraint.

The cemetery was closed in 1903, and by then, it contained some 300 graves. One can view it from behind a fence, but a special visit can also be arranged, though now it is also included in a Royal Parks guided tour.

4. The Sherlock Holmes Pub

The Sherlock Holmes Pub is a public house with a Victorian era theme, located in Northumberland Street, near Trafalgar Square and the Charing Cross railway station. While it is certainly not the only Sherlock Holmes pub in the world, it is notable for one thing - the large collection of memorabilia related to the iconic fictional detective created by Sir Arthur Conan Doyle.

Originally, this pub was a small hotel - known as Northumberland Hotel, and then later on as the Northumberland Arms. Some have even speculated that this is the same Northumberland Hotel that was mentioned in The Hound of the Baskervilles. The name

Northumberland Arms, in fact, did appear in the story The Adventure of the Noble Bachelor.

In 1951, during the Festival of Britain, the Marylebone Public Library, and Abbey National (who had its headquarters at 221B Baker Street), created an exhibition celebrating the fictional detective. The collection was put together with the help of enthusiasts, and also the support of the family of Sir Arthur Conan Doyle. Then, when the Northumberland Arms was refurbished in 1957, they were able to purchase the entire collection - after it came home from a world tour. The pub was restored to a Victorian era theme, and the collection was featured inside as an exhibit - including a detailed replica of a corner of Holmes' apartment. To some, it almost feels like Holmes and Watson can step in at any moment.

Everything you can probably think of relating to many of the detective's varied adventures - is featured in the pub - including his violin, pipe, scientific equipment, and Dr. Watson's service revolver. Fans of the intrepid detective can have a magnificent time identifying these various curio and recalling their significance in the fictional detective's life and exploits. Today, the place also includes photographs of the many different actors who have played Holmes and his partner Watson throughout the years.

And of course, it is a good place to sit down and have a pint.

5. *London Beer Gardens*

A beer garden is precisely that - outdoor seating amidst lush greenery, where they serve - not coffee, not tea - but beer.

There are a good number of beer gardens in London, and people who congregate to these places do so in common appreciation of good weather, quiet and beautiful surroundings, and wonderful beer.

While not precisely what you may call hidden, these small spots of garden oasis are usually frequented by locals, and not commonly included in London tours which focus more on historic or unique pubs. The atmosphere is completed by a bucolic atmosphere and even some barbecue food. Many are located riverside, which only serves to complete their serene and peaceful surroundings. After all, who said that drinking beer should be limited to nightly activities amidst low-lit rooms and loud music? Beer goes just as well with sunshine, laughter, a laid-back atmosphere, fresh air, and lush foliage, too. Since beer gardens have begun to grow in popularity, rooftops bar have also begun making an appearance - open-air bars on building rooftops, where the greenery has been suitably replaced with amazing views.

Here are a few to get you started:

- Spaniards Inn, at Hampstead Heath
- the Stag at Fleed Road
- the Faltering Fullback at Camden
- The Jam Tree in Chelsea
- The Candlemaker at Clapham
- The Fentiman Arms - Geronimo Inns at Vauxhall
- Rolling Stock at Shoreditch
- the Gorringe Park at Wandsworth
- the Garden Gate at Finsbury Park
- The Wood House at Sydenham
- The Aeronaut in Acton
- The Old Brewery in Greenwich
- the Cambria near the Loughborough Junction Station

6. *The Jewel Tower*

The Jewel Tower at Westminster was built between 1365 to 1366, for the purpose of housing the personal treasures of Edward III - an accummulation of a vast collection of jewels and plates. And it did serve this purpose for a time - occupying a secluded part in the southwest of the Palace of Westminster, protected by a moat that was linked to the River Thames. Technically, however, the tower was built on land that was owned by the Westminster Abbey. It took six years before the King agreed to compensate the monks for this.

In 1512, a fire broke out in the Palace, and the then-king Henry VIII relocated to Whitehall. The tower was still used as storage for various royal furniture and household effects. In 1590, it was also used to store parliamentary records - when it was termed the Parliament Office rather than the Jewel Tower. It was renovated in 1621 for this purpose - increasing its fire protection.

Over the next few years, the tower fell into ruin. The moat that surrounded it gradually filled up, and despite many subsquent renovations and repairs, it was simply unsuitable for habitation, storage, and even its capacity to withstand fire. It was completely obscured by the surrounding buildings, and could only be accessed through the office in front of it.

Then in 1834, another fire swept through Westminster, and most of the old palace was destroyed. It is only one of four structures of the original palace that survived the fire - others include Westminster Hall, the Cloisters and Chapter House of St. Stephen, and the Chapel of St. Mary's Undercroft. Since then, people again started calling it the Jewel Tower.

Some of the notable features of the Jewel Tower include the ornate carved ceiling carvings, the history of weights and measures, alongside over 400 objects that were associated with the tower.

It was opened to the public as a tourist attraction in the 21st century, but it has proven a challenging site to operate given the capacity constraints and weather conditions such as heat and humidity, so not very many people know about it. It is, however, a worthy site to visit - remaining virtually unaltered to this day.

7. Jack the Ripper Tour

FINDING ᴛʜᴇ MUTILATED BODY IN MITRE SQARE

Hankering after something a bit more dark and sinister? Or perhaps you are just fascinated by crime, mystery, and unsolved history? Various groups in London are offering a tour of the city with a focus on one of the most notorious Londoner of all: Jack the Ripper.

The real identity of serial killer Jack the Ripper is unknown to this day. Sometimes also referred to as the "Whitechapel Murderer" and the "Leather Apron," the man was known for his brutal murder and mutilation of prostitutes in the East End of London sometime in 1888. His fame was solidified by the "canonical five" - five murders in Whitechapel which were linked because of the particular brutality and viciousness of the attacks.

These murders were never solved, and now have become the subject of genuine historical research and over hundreds of speculation. It is a genuine, unsolved mystery, and to this day, study and analysis of the case files is referred to as "ripperology."

Depending on which tour you join, you will be conducted through the streets and byways of London, under the guide of a historical expert knowledgeable about the different theories and suspicions regarding what happened and who Jack really was. It can be a fascinating and absorbing tour - especially as you make your way through London at night, while hearing the stories of the actual murders that took place during the Autumn of Terror. It does serve to capture the imagination - not only for the shock value of what transpired all those years ago, but also because it was all based on truth.

8. *Thames Barrier*

The Thames Barrier was built and became fully operational in 1982 on the Thames, at the eastern side of Woolwich capital. It was designed to protect over 48 sq miles (125 sq km) of central London from flooding due to tidal surges and rainfall swelling. That's responsibility for an estimated 1.25 million people, and over £200 billion worth of propery and infrastructure. It is well worth a visit - there is an exhibition and a working scale model for visitors that would help people understand how the Barrier works.

It is ranked the second largest flood defence barrier in the world, after the Oosterscheldekering barrier in the Netherlands. It spans 520 meters across the Thames, and features 10 steel gates which are over 20 m high, and weighs

3,700 tons each - they are capable of withstanding an overload of more than 9,000 tons of water.

Depending on the threat of flooding - which are monitored by forecasting systems and computer models, the Thames Barrier can either be partially (underspill) or fully closed, thus regulating the volume of water that can move up the river from the sea. While each gate can be closed in ten minutes - it takes around an hour and a half for the whole barrier to close completely. They are only reopened again when the water level upstream and downstream match. When they are not in use,they are hidden out of sight in curved recessed concrete cills in the riverbed, among which river traffic can pass through.

It took around 8 years, at a cost of £500 million to construct the Thames River Barrier - this was prompted by previous cases of flooding in London that claimed people's lives. London is a flood-prone area; in 1928, 14 people died when the Thames flooded. During this time, the only accepted solution was to build higher and stronger river walls and embankments. But after 307 people died in the North Sea flood of 1953, the flood issue was revisited.

While its effectivity is expected to decline over time (its lifespan is estimated to last only until 2030), it has proven its use in past years. As of March 2014, it was estimated to have been closed 174 times to protect against flooding. Estimates say that it might prove itself sufficient protection against flooding well until 2070.

9. *Dennis Sever's House*

At 18 Folgate Street in Spitalfields stands the old house of artist Severs - one of a terrace of houses, with red brick dressings and comprises four storeys and a basement. It may seem like just a regular house, but once you step inside, you are transported completely to another world.

Some call the interior of the house a still life in 3D, others a time capsule, and still others an exercise in obsessiveness. What Dennis Severs did was to create within the ten rooms of the house an imaginary atmosphere that invites you to imagine that the 18th century family of

Huguenot silk-weavers live there, have just stepped outside for a moment, and might return at any instant.

It is a strange collection of a variety of sights, smells, sounds, and even lighting, that adds to this strange atmosphere - from half-eaten bread, to beds still unmade that have just been slept in, and things left behind. The motto of the house is "You either see it or you don't." (*Aut Visum Aut Non!*). If you do have an imagination vivid enough to imagine a fictional family simply from a made-up atmosphere inside the house, this can be a strange, even a haunting visit - and a unique glimpse into the lives of another era.

While the house is open to the public, visitors are asked to respect the creator's intent. It's probably not advisable to bring kids along for this visit, as the tours are conducted in silence.

10. *Queen Elizabeth's Hunting Lodge*

The Queen Elizabeth's Hunting Lodge is situation on the edge of Epping Forest, in Chingford, London, at the London Borough of Waltham Forest, and near Greater London's boundary with Essex.

The building was originally known as the Great Standing - built by order of Henry VIII in 1542-1543 to serve as an open-sided viewing platform from which guests could view the hunt, and even shoot deer from the upper floors. The windows we see today were only installed later, after the reign of Charles I. It was renovated further in 1589 for Queen Elizabeth I. Today, it has been opened as a museum that is open to all.

The former lodge is a timber-framed, three-storey building that features a unique Tudor kitchen wtih food and kitchenware. In the upper floors and displays of costumes and carpentry joints from Tudor times. Various activities such as dressing up in costumes and following a quiz trail is available for childreen. One can have a magificent view of the surrounding Chingford Plain and Epping Forest, and tours also include various other stories of the house, the forest and the surroundings, including the stairs up which it was said that Queen Elizabeth rode her horse.

A visit to this area is a magnificent chance to relax, unwind in beautiful surroundings, and spend a enjoyable and leisurely time with family. The surrounding Epping Forest also offers various activities such as jogging, horse riding, or cycling.

The site itself is central to many Tudor-themed events and festivals each year, so it would be great to check their schedule beforehand to see if there are any upcoming events that would surely add another dimension to your visit!

Chapter Ten: Conclusion

The lists of various sights and attractions we have presented to you in this book is by no means comprehensive or exhaustive - London is a historical and cultural marvel, and there are always a few more sights and places to see. It is one of the most visited places in the world, and there is always one thing or another that we have not seen before. It is hoped, however, that the information presented to you in this book would help you get off to a good start.

As you prepare yourself for your visit to London, plan carefully and well. Below are a few tips and guidelines to keep in mind. But always remember that in the end, the places we visit do tend to end up guiding us in our explorations.

And of course, don't forget to stay safe!

- Make copies and backups of your passport and credit card information and store them in a safe place - should your cards get stolen or lost, it's always a good idea to have copies of them for cancellations or new applications.

- Plan your itinerary beforehand - not only does this allow you to choose the most convenient hotel, and figure out how to get from one point to another, but it will also allow you to make the most of your trip. That said, don't discount or ignore the occasional pleasant surprise that often does happens during travels.

- Pack the essentials: a small medical kit, especially if you're prone to an illness or two, snack bags, universal chargers and plug adapters, folding bags for packing souvenirs and other stuff you might pick up at London's local markets, and digital gear to help you store your memories while in London. Try not to pack too much gear, however - nor ones that are too bulky.

- In terms of clothing it's probably best to bring clothes that you can layer. It's not unheard of to experience snow, rain and sunshine all in one afternoon - layering clothes allows you to remove or add a few at a time to help you adjust more conveniently to temperature changes. And keep to neutral colors - this would help you blend in with the locals who generally seem to prefer dark, sombre colors. And don't forget to pick comfortable shoes that are also waterproof - there will likely be a number of times when you'll find yourself walking along the sidewalk when it is raining! And whichever the season, having a folded umbrella secreted in your bag is essential.

- Don't forget to bring a map, to help you get around. If you know that you're going to be commuting around the city a lot during your stay, you might want to get an Oyster Card - these are smartcards you can use instead of paper tickets for buses, the Tube, trams, DLR, Underground, the Rail, and most National Rail Services in London - for discounted rates! It's also pretty convenient since all you really have to do is swipe them.

- Read up on local customs as much as you can - not only can this help you in navigating your way around their unique culture and lifestyle, this also helps you avoid instances of miscommunication and confusion. And more important - it helps you preserve a sense of common courtesy to local customs and traditions.

- Practice the general rules of safety. London is safe, as a general rule - but that doesn't mean you should push against its limits, either. Don't do drugs; don't drink if you're underage, and get good insurance coverage that you will be able to use in London hospitals.

London Quick Travel Guide

1. *London Quick Facts*
    a. Currency - The pound sterling (£/GBP)
    b. Primary Language spoken: English
    c. Weather and seasons - unpredictable, but rarely extreme
       - Spring - March, April and May; expect sudden rain showers
       - Summer - March, April and May; average temperatures are 9-18 degrees Celsius (48-64 degrees Fahrenheit)
       - Autumn - June, July and August; either mild and dry or wet and windy

- Winter - December, January and February; average of 2-7 degrees Celsius (36 degrees Fahrenheit)

    d. Tourist seasons - pretty much year round, but late spring and summer is usually the prime tourist season

2. *Transportation*

Points of Entry Into London:

a. Airports
- Heathrow Airport (Hilingdon)
- Gatwick Airport (West Sussex)
- Stansted Airport (Essex)
- Luton Airport (Bedfordshire)
- London City Airport (Newham, East London)

b. Ferry Services
- These operate regularly for passengers and vehicles traveling to and from the UK, continental Europe, and Ireland

c. By Train
- Victoria Station (from Dover and Newhaven)
- Liverpool Street Station (terminus for Harwich services)
- London Euston Station (links with Holyhead)
- London Paddington Station (interchange at Cardiff Central)

d. Eurotunnel and Eurostar

- Eurotunnel provides high-speed car, coach and freight shuttle services via the Challel Tunnel
- Eurostar is a good value rail-service running via the Channel Tunnel

e. By Road
- The UK and London has an extensive motorway network; all of London's motorways intersect the M25 orbital motorway.

Getting Around Within London

- Bus
- Cable car
- Cycling
- Port and Riverboats
- By Car (remember to drive on the left!)
- By Cab
- Via the Underground Railway
- Walking

Index

D

E

F

G

H

J

K

L

M

N

O

P

T

U

Photo References

Page 1 Photo by chafleks via Pixabay.
<https://pixabay.com/en/london-city-london-city-england-1018629/>

Page 12 Photo by Umezo KAMATA via Wikimedia Commons.
<https://commons.wikimedia.org/wiki/File:06LSE,BBC,Kingsway.jpg>

Page 14 Photo by User: Mahlum.
<https://commons.wikimedia.org/wiki/File:Bloomsbury_Street_London.jpg>

Page 15 Photo by Thomas Nugent via Wikimedia Commons.
<https://commons.wikimedia.org/wiki/File:Addington_Street_-_geograph.org.uk_-_1708190.jpg>

Page 17 Photo by Stephen McKay via Wikimedia Commons.
<https://commons.wikimedia.org/wiki/File:Victoria_Street,_Westminster_-_geograph.org.uk_-_437704.jpg>

Page 18 Photo by Хомелка via Wikimedia Commons.
<https://commons.wikimedia.org/wiki/File:Unidentified_in_the_City_of_London_46.JPG>

Page 20 Photo by Sardaka via Wikimedia Commons.
<https://commons.wikimedia.org/wiki/File:(1)William_Street_Kings_Cross.jpg>

Page 23 Photo by Ghouston via Wikimedia Commons.
<https://commons.wikimedia.org/wiki/File:Kensington-high-street-20060330-029.jpg>

Page 25 Photo by Betty Longbottom via Wikimedia Commons.
<https://commons.wikimedia.org/wiki/File:Bayswater_Terrace_-_Bayswater_View_-_geograph.org.uk_-_1129512.jpg>

Page 26 Photo by Philafrenzy via Wikimedia Commons.
<https://commons.wikimedia.org/wiki/File:Paddington_Street,_London_W1.JPG>

Page 28 Photo by Chris Eason via Wikimedia Commons.
<https://commons.wikimedia.org/wiki/File:Canary_Wharf_(8132597075).jpg>

Page 32 Photo by Lewis Clarke via Wikimedia Commons.
<https://commons.wikimedia.org/wiki/File:London_,_Westminster_-_Regent_Street_-_geograph.org.uk_-_1738922.jpg>

Page 34 Photo by Philafrenzy via Wikimedia Commons.
<https://commons.wikimedia.org/wiki/File:Knightsbridge_20_Sept_2015.JPG>

Page 36 Photo by Henry Kellner via Wikimeda Commons.
<https://en.wikipedia.org/wiki/File:COVENT_GARDEN_MARKET_BUILDING_7482_pano_12.jpg>

Page 37 Photo by Ysangkok via Wikimedia Commons. <https://commons.wikimedia.org/wiki/File:Oxford_Street _December_2006.jpeg>

Page 39 Photo by SisterLondon via Wikimedia Commons. <https://commons.wikimedia.org/wiki/File:Carnaby_Lon don.jpg>

Page 40 Photo by Mark Ahsmann via Wikimedia Commons. <https://commons.wikimedia.org/wiki/File:King%27s_Ro ad,_Chelsea,_London_SW10,_4_June_2011.jpg>

Page 42 Photo by Russell Trebor via Wikimedia Commons. <https://commons.wikimedia.org/wiki/File:Fulham_Broa dway_-_geograph.org.uk_-_313307.jpg>

Page 44 Photo by CGP Grey (http://www.cgpgrey.com) via Wikimedia Commons. <https://commons.wikimedia.org/wiki/File:2005-11-12_- _London_-_Camden_Town_- _jewellery_(4887830999).jpg>

Page 46 Photo by Surgeonsmate at English Wikipedia via Wikimedia Commons. <https://commons.wikimedia.org/wiki/File:OldandNewB ondStreet.JPG>

Page 48 Photo by Panhard via Wikimedia Commons. <https://commons.wikimedia.org/wiki/File:Westfield_Lo ndon_028.jpg>

Page 52 Photo by Public Domain Images via Pixabay. <https://pixabay.com/en/england-london-museum-british-387316/>

Page 55 Photo by Cjc13 via Wikimedia Commons. <https://commons.wikimedia.org/wiki/File:Bankside_Power_Station.jpg>

Page 58 Photo by Tony Hisgett via Wikimedia Commons. <https://en.wikipedia.org/wiki/File:Tate_Britain_(5822081512)_(2).jpg>

Page 60 Photo by drdevience via Pixabay. <https://pixabay.com/en/united-kingdom-england-london-89977/>

Page 62 Photo by Ham via Wikimedia Commons. <https://commons.wikimedia.org/wiki/File:London_NPG.JPG>

Page 64 Photo by Adrian Pingstone via Wikimedia Commons. <https://commons.wikimedia.org/wiki/File:Nat.hist.mus.exterior.arp.jpg>

Page 67 Photo by David Castor via Wikimedia Commons. <https://commons.wikimedia.org/wiki/File:Victoria_and_Albert_Museum-1.jpg>

Page 69 Photo by Christine Matthews via Wikimedia Commons. <https://commons.wikimedia.org/wiki/File:Science_Muse

um,_Exhibition_Road,_London_SW7_-
geograph.org.uk-_1125595.jpg>

Page 71 Photo by Katie Chan via Wikimedia Commons.
<https://commons.wikimedia.org/wiki/File:EH1211481_N
ational_Maritime_Museum_10.JPG>

Page 73 Photo by Infernalfox via Wikimedia Commons.
<https://commons.wikimedia.org/wiki/File:Museum_of_
London.jpg>

Page 76 Photo by skeeze via Pixabay.
<https://pixabay.com/en/big-ben-close-up-landmark-
london-1034661/>

Page 79 Photo by Stevebidmead via Pixabay.
<https://pixabay.com/en/westminster-palace-of-
westminster-347972/>

Page 83 Photo by Ceaton89 via Wikipedia.
<https://commons.wikimedia.org/wiki/File:Westminster_
Abbey_-_Nov_2013.jpg>

Page 86 Photo by Gic via Pixabay.
<https://pixabay.com/en/tower-of-london-tower-london-
948978/>

Page 88 Photo by fotofan1 via Pixabay.
<https://pixabay.com/en/london-tower-bridge-bridge-
monument-441853/>

Page 92 Photo by siegertmarc via Wikimedia Commons. <https://commons.wikimedia.org/wiki/File:CWR_Entranc e_(6017503540).jpg>

Page 95 Photo by Mark Fosh via Wikimedia Commons, as uploaded by Nanonic. <https://commons.wikimedia.org/wiki/File:St_Pauls_aeri al_(cropped).jpg>

Page 98 RodneyBamford via Pixabay. <https://pixabay.com/en/hampton-court-palace-palace-hampton-541081/>

Page 101 Photo by 3BRBS via Wikimedia Commons. <https://commons.wikimedia.org/wiki/File:Guildhall_%2 B_Roman_amphitheatre_on_the_Guildhall_Yard_-_Left_Side_Panorama_02.jpg>

Page 103 Photo by jeffwallis via Pixabay. <https://pixabay.com/en/cutty-sark-ship-london-historic-1369026/>

Page 107 Photo by Witizia via Pixabay. <https://pixabay.com/en/london-eye-london-city-england-351203/>

Page 111 Photo by dgazdik via Pixabay. <https://pixabay.com/en/london-hyde-park-1517309/>

Page 114 Photo by Cristian Bortes via Wikimedia Images. <https://commons.wikimedia.org/wiki/File:Autumn_in_S t._James_Park_-_London_(4047159621).jpg>

Page 116 Photo by Another Believer via Wikimeda
Commons.
<https://commons.wikimedia.org/wiki/File:Kensington_
Gardens,_London_(2014)_-_3.JPG>

Page 118 Photo by tpsdave via Pixabay.
<https://pixabay.com/en/london-england-trafalgar-
square-123785/>

Page 120 Photo by Patche99z via Wikimedia Commons.
<https://commons.wikimedia.org/wiki/File:Kew_Gardens
_Palm_House_6248.JPG>

Page 122 Photo by Laika ac via Wikimedia Commons.
<https://commons.wikimedia.org/wiki/File:Highgate_Ce
metery_(20414246764).jpg>

Page 124 Photo by dconvertini via Wikimedia Commons.
<https://commons.wikimedia.org/wiki/File:DSC6048_-
Flickr-_dconvertini.jpg>

Page 126 Photo by Tony Hisgett via Wikimedia Commons.
<https://commons.wikimedia.org/wiki/File:St_Pauls_and
_Millenium_Bridge_bw_(5653923162).jpg>

Page 128 Photo by Skitterphoto via Pixabay.
<https://pixabay.com/en/london-piccadilly-circus-
england-1365339/>

Page 131 Photo by Kenneth Allen via Wikimedia Commons.
<https://commons.wikimedia.org/wiki/File:Changing_of_
the_Guards,_Windsor_-_geograph.org.uk_-_908764.jpg>

Page 133 Photo by Crochet.david via Wikimedia Commons. <https://commons.wikimedia.org/wiki/File:Le_Royal_Mews_de_Londres-018.JPG>

Page 134 Photo by Gripweed via Wikimedia Commons. <https://commons.wikimedia.org/wiki/File:London_Dungeon.JPG>

Page 136 Photo by Jim Linwood via flickr. <https://www.flickr.com/photos/brighton/7180684678/>

Page 138 Photo by Mike Fleming via Wikimedia Images. <https://commons.wikimedia.org/wiki/File:Regent%27s_Park_open_air_theatre.jpg>

Page 139 Photo by SkErDi&Ana via Wikimedia Commons. <https://commons.wikimedia.org/wiki/File:Madame_Tussauds_London.jpg>

Page 142 Photo by Nigel Cox via Wikimedia Commons. <https://commons.wikimedia.org/wiki/File:Spitalfields_City_Farm,_Buxton_Street,_E1_-_geograph.org.uk_-_785986.jpg>

Page 144 Photo by gailf548 via Wikimedia Commons. <https://commons.wikimedia.org/wiki/File:221b_Baker_Street_Placa.jpg>

Page 146 Photo by Zenior via Wikimedia Commons. <https://commons.wikimedia.org/wiki/File:London-traditional-pub-westminster-beer.jpg>

Page 148 Photo by Mariordo (Mario Roberto Durán Ortiz) via Wikimedia Commons.
<https://commons.wikimedia.org/wiki/File:London_01_2013_The_Shard_5462.JPG>

Page 151 Photo by Adrian Pingstone via Wikimedia Commons.
<https://commons.wikimedia.org/wiki/File:Yeoman.warder.toweroflondon.arp.jpg>

Page 154 Photo by Editor 1000 via Wikimedia Commons.
<https://commons.wikimedia.org/wiki/File:Hairsprayoct07.jpg>

Page 156 Photo by tpsdave via Pixabay.
<https://pixabay.com/en/theatre-stage-crowd-people-91882/>

Page 158 Photo by Richard Giddins via Wikimedia Commons.
<https://commons.wikimedia.org/wiki/File:Pteropus_poliocephalus_Sydney_BG.jpg>

Page 159 Photo by D1MK via Pixabay.
<https://pixabay.com/en/moon-stars-sky-night-dark-galaxy-1524783/>

Page 161 Photo by Mark Ahsmann via Wikimedia Commons.
<https://commons.wikimedia.org/wiki/File:Up_the_Creek_comedy_club,_London_SE10.jpg>

Page 163 Photo by Andy MacLarty via Wikimedia Commons, as uploaded by Bryan. <https://commons.wikimedia.org/wiki/File:U2_Live8_Hyde_Park.jpg>

Page 165 Photo by LilaTretikov via Wikimedia Commons. <https://commons.wikimedia.org/wiki/File:The_Britania_Pub.jpg>

Page 166 Photo by Grim23 via Wikimeda Commons. <https://commons.wikimedia.org/wiki/File:Matter_dance floor_2009.JPG>

Page 168 Photo by JFKennedy at English Wikipedia, via Wikimedia Commons. <https://commons.wikimedia.org/wiki/File:London_Night_view.jpg>

Page 172 Photo by Brian Harrington Spier via Wikimedia Commons. <https://commons.wikimedia.org/wiki/File:London%27s_Secrets-_6_Aug_12_(7751562676).jpg>

Page 175 Photo by John Salmon via Wikimedia Commons. <https://commons.wikimedia.org/wiki/File:The_Hardy_Tree,_St_Pancras_(Old_Church),_Churchyard_-_geograph.org.uk_-_1507169.jpg>

Page 177 Photo by Pedro Cambra via Flickr. <https://www.flickr.com/photos/pcambra/4484429110/>

Page 179 Photo by Danny Choo from Tokyo, Japan via
Wikimedia Commons.
<https://commons.wikimedia.org/wiki/File:Milky_Holme
s_in_London_(5080111841).jpg>

Page 181 Photo by Ewan Munro from London, UK via
Wikimedia Commons.
<https://commons.wikimedia.org/wiki/File:Cambria,_Lo
ughborough_Junction,_SE5_(3835203630).jpg>

Page 183 Photo by Elisa.rolle via Wikimedia Commons.
<https://commons.wikimedia.org/wiki/File:The_Jewel_H
ouse,_2001.jpg>

Page 185 Photo by unknown via Wikimedia Commons.
<https://commons.wikimedia.org/wiki/File:Illustrated_Po
lice_News_-_Jack_the_Ripper_2.png>

Page 187 Photo by Peter Trimming via Wikimedia
Commons.
<https://commons.wikimedia.org/wiki/File:Thames_Barri
er_-_geograph.org.uk_-_1466865.jpg>

Page 189 Photo by Matt Brown via Wikimedia Commons.
<https://commons.wikimedia.org/wiki/File:Dennis_Sever
s_House_(15290690150).jpg>

Page 191 Photo by Stephen McKay via Wikimedia
Commons.
<https://commons.wikimedia.org/wiki/File:Queen_Elizab

eth%27s_Hunting_Lodge_-_geograph.org.uk_-
_1524048.jpg>

Page 193 Photo by Pexels via Pixabay.
<https://pixabay.com/en/black-and-white-traffic-red-
street-1283853/>

Page 197 Photo by Adrian Pingstone via Wikimedia
Commons.
<https://commons.wikimedia.org/wiki/File:Virgin_atlanti
c_b747-400_g-vbig_arp.jpg>

References

"10 Facts about Piccadilly Circus you may not know." Matt
Gedge. <https://funlondontours.com/news/10-facts-
about-piccadilly-circus-you-may-not-know>

"10 of the best clubs in London." Wil Troup.
<https://www.theguardian.com/travel/2011/may/06/top-
10-clubs-london-nightlife>

"11 Secrets of Piccadilly Circus." Laura Reynolds.
<http://londonist.com/2016/05/secrets-of-piccadilly-
circus>

"17 Top-Rated Tourist Attractions in London." Bryan
Dearsley. <http://www.planetware.com/tourist-
attractions-/london-eng-l-lon.htm>

"17 Things To Do on a Cheap Night Out in London."
VisitLondom.com. <http://www.visitlondon.com/things-
to-do/nightlife/17-things-to-do-on-a-cheap-night-out-in-
london#ULpd2IIKpKS7jr9b.97>

"18 of the best live music venues in London." World Travel
Guide.
<http://www.worldtravelguide.net/holidays/editorial-
feature/feature/18-best-live-music-venues-london>

"221B Baker Street." Wikipedia.
<https://en.wikipedia.org/wiki/221B_Baker_Street>

"5 Facts About Tower Bridge." History Extra. <http://www.historyextra.com/article/victorians/5-facts-about-tower-bridge>

"A Timeline of London History." Tim Lambert. <http://www.localhistories.org/londontime.html>

"A Tour of London's Roman Amphiteatre." Hannah Collingbourne. <http://blog.visitlondon.com/2010/03/a-tour-of-londons-roman-amphitheatre/>

"Baker Street." Wikipedia. <https://en.wikipedia.org/wiki/Baker_Street>

"Bat Walk in Kensington Gardens." London Community Resource Network." <http://lcrn.org.uk/bat-walk-kensington-gardens/>

"Bat Walking Tour." The Royal Parks. <https://www.royalparks.org.uk/parks/hyde-park/things-to-see-and-do/events-in-hyde-park/upcoming-events-in-hyde-park/bat-walking-tour>

"Bayswater." Wikipedia. <https://en.wikipedia.org/wiki/Bayswater>

"Beer Gardens in London." designmynight. <https://www.designmynight.com/london/pubs/beer-gardens-in-london>

"Best outdoor cinemas in the UK: Where to watch films outside in London and beyond over summer 2016." Jess

Denham. <http://www.independent.co.uk/arts-
entertainment/films/features/best-outdoor-cinemas-uk-
london-where-to-watch-films-outside-2016-luna-cinema-
somerset-house-rooftop-a7062026.html>

"Best Times to Visit London." US News & World Report.
<http://travel.usnews.com/London_England/When_To_V
isit/>

"Big Ben." a view on cities.
<http://www.aviewoncities.com/london/bigben.htm>

"Big Ben." Wikipedia.
<https://en.wikipedia.org/wiki/Big_Ben#Cultural_import
ance>

"Big Brands and Museum Stores: Shop Your Socks Off in
Knightsbridge." Emma Wallis.
<http://www.10best.com/destinations/uk-
england/london/shopping/knightsbridges-best/>

"Bloomsbury." Wikipedia.
<https://en.wikipedia.org/wiki/Bloomsbury#Parks_and_s
quares>

"Bond Street." VisitLondon.com.
<http://www.visitlondon.com/things-to-
do/place/7883674-bond-street#Aajq2YAwfF3Uge0E.97>

"Bond Street." Wikipedia.
<https://en.wikipedia.org/wiki/Bond_Street>

"British Museum." Lauralee Davies.
<http://www.timeout.com/london/museums/british-museum>

"British Museum." Wikipedia.
<https://en.wikipedia.org/wiki/British_Museum#Disputed_items_in_the_collection>

"Broadway Market." Hackney.
<http://www.hackney.gov.uk/broadway-market>

"Broadway Market." Wikipedia.
<https://en.wikipedia.org/wiki/Broadway_Market>

"Broadway Market: an insider's guide." Dan Jones.
<http://www.timeout.com/london/shopping/broadway-market-guide>

"Buckingham Palace." A View on the Cities.
<http://www.aviewoncities.com/london/buckinghampalace.htm>

"Camden Town." Wikipedia.
<https://en.wikipedia.org/wiki/Camden_Town#Landmarks>

"Canary Wharf." Wikipedia.
<https://en.wikipedia.org/wiki/Canary_Wharf>

"Carnaby Street, 1960's London." historypin.org.
<https://www.historypin.org/attach/uid25519/tours/view/id/1921/title/Carnaby%20Street,%201960's%20London.>

"Carnaby Street." VisitLondon.com.
    <http://www.visitlondon.com/things-to-do/place/46455-
    carnaby-street#Bt3UWXmSej8xOZed.97>

"Carnaby Street." Wikipedia.
    <https://en.wikipedia.org/wiki/Carnaby_Street>

"Ceremony of the Keys." Trooping the Colour.
    <http://www.trooping-the-colour.co.uk/keys/>

"Ceremony of the Keys at the Tower of London." About
    Travel.
    <http://golondon.about.com/od/londonforfree/fr/Ceremo
    nyoftheKeys.htm>

"Ceremony of the Keys." Wikipedia.
    <https://en.wikipedia.org/wiki/Ceremony_of_the_Keys>

"Changing the Guard." The Household Division.
    <http://www.householddivision.org.uk/changing-the-
    guard>

"Changing the Guard at Buckingham Palace." Visit
    London.com. <http://www.visitlondon.com/things-to-
    do/event/8725947-changing-the-
    guard#ujy2tMXbU2z9zWy2.97>

"Churchill War Rooms." Lauralee Davies.
    <http://www.timeout.com/london/museums/churchill-
    war-rooms>

"Churchill War Rooms." Wikipedia.
    <https://en.wikipedia.org/wiki/Churchill_War_Rooms>

"City Farms in London." Things To Do Editors.
    <http://www.timeout.com/london/things-to-do/city-
    farms-in-london>

"City of London." Wikipedia.
    <https://en.wikipedia.org/wiki/City_of_London>

"County Hall, London." Wikipedia.
    <https://en.wikipedia.org/wiki/County_Hall,_London>

"Covent Garden." VisitLondon.com.
    <http://www.visitlondon.com/things-to-do/london-
    areas/covent-garden#a09CpBKPUh2whG1t.97>

"Covent Garden." Wikipedia.
    <https://en.wikipedia.org/wiki/Covent_Garden>

"Cutty Sark." Royal Museums Greenwich.
    <http://www.rmg.co.uk/cutty-sark>

"Cutty Sark." VisitLondon.com.
    <http://www.visitlondon.com/things-to-do/place/197352-
    cutty-sark-greenwich#l8iS0kwZvPPrYJg7.97>

"Cutty Sark." Wikipedia.
    <https://en.wikipedia.org/wiki/Cutty_Sark#Museum_shi
    p>

"Dennis Sever's House." TimeOut.
    <http://www.timeout.com/london/attractions/dennis-
    severs-house>

"Dennis Sever's House." Wikipedia.
    <https://en.wikipedia.org/wiki/Dennis_Severs%27_House
    >

"Dennis Sever's House." VisitLondon.com.
    <http://www.visitlondon.com/things-to-do/place/50657-
    dennis-severs-house#lwoRYVfmPbSp6P4J.97>

"Dining on Regent Street." Regent Street.
    <http://www.regentstreetonline.com/zeitgeist/dining-on-
    regent-street>

"Discover Hyde Park's dark secrets." The Royal Parks
    Foundation.
    <http://www.supporttheroyalparks.org/about_us/news/1
    479_discover_hyde_park_s_dark_secrets>

"Exploring The Ancient Church And Burial Ground of Old
    St Pancras." Flickering Lamps.
    <https://flickeringlamps.com/2014/07/20/exploring-the-
    ancient-church-and-burial-ground-of-old-st-pancras/>

"Ferry Connections to London." VisitLondon.com.
    <http://www.visitlondon.com/traveller-
    information/travel-to-
    london/ferry#XOdGFOrdLFdeEJBp.97>

"Getting to London by Car and Motorcycle." VisitLondon.com. <http://www.visitlondon.com/traveller-information/travel-to-london/london-car-and-motorcycle#0IIlfgQEIFFhzK0f.97>

"Guide to Hotel Districts of Central London." The London Toolkit. <https://www.londontoolkit.com/accommodation/london_hotel_briefing.htm>

"Guildhall Art Gallery." Wikipedia. <https://en.wikipedia.org/wiki/Guildhall_Art_Gallery>

"Guildhall Art Gallery & Roman Amphiteatre." Visit London.com. <http://www.visitlondon.com/things-to-do/place/157999-guildhall-art-gallery-and-roman-amphitheatre#8zZkRR8KTpDVsFUb.97>

"Guildhall's Underground Roman Amphiteater." Atlas Obscura. <http://www.atlasobscura.com/places/guildhall-underground-amphitheater>

"Hampstead Observatory." TimeOut. <http://www.timeout.com/london/things-to-do/hampstead-observatory-1>

"Hampton Court Palace." Visit London.com. <http://www.visitlondon.com/things-to-do/place/427279-hampton-court-palace#vp5MHKGZ9ieZAoIQ.97>

"Hampton Court Palace." Wikipedia.
    <https://en.wikipedia.org/wiki/Hampton_Court_Palace>

"Hans Sloane." Wikipedia.
    <https://en.wikipedia.org/wiki/Hans_Sloane>

"Highgate Cemetery." Atlas Obscura.
    <http://www.atlasobscura.com/places/highgate-
    cemetery>

"Highgate Cemetery." VisitLondon.com.
    <http://www.visitlondon.com/things-to-do/place/149369-
    highgate-cemetery#7c1Duiteod3HcaYP.97>

"Highgate Cemetery." Wikipedia.
    <https://en.wikipedia.org/wiki/Highgate_Cemetery>

"History of the Cutty Sark." History.
    <http://www.history.co.uk/shows/cutty-
    sark/articles/history-of-the-cutty-sark>

"History of London." Wikipedia.
    <https://en.wikipedia.org/wiki/History_of_London>

"Hotels Near Canary Wharf London Docklands." The
    London Toolkit.
    <https://www.londontoolkit.com/accommodation/canary
    _wharf_hotels.html>

"House Music Clubs in London." design my night.
    <https://www.designmynight.com/london/clubs/house-
    music-clubs-in-london>

"How does the Thames Barrier stop London Flooding?" Tom de Castella. <http://www.bbc.com/news/magazine-26133660>

"How Much Do You Really Know About Trafalgar Square?" Londonist. <http://londonist.com/2015/03/how-much-do-you-really-know-about-trafalgar-square>

"Hyde Park." A View on Cities. <http://www.aviewoncities.com/london/hydepark.htm>

"Hyde Park." The Royal Parks. <https://www.royalparks.org.uk/parks/hyde-park>

"Hyde Park." VisitLondon.com. <http://www.visitlondon.com/things-to-do/place/610718-hyde-park#6XTTkhKoGILOoFDA.97>

"Hyde Park, London." Wikipedia. <https://en.wikipedia.org/wiki/Hyde_Park,_London>

"Hyde Park Pet Cemetery." Atlas Obscura. <http://www.atlasobscura.com/places/hyde-park-pet-cemetery>

"If we can't rest in peace, handle with care." Philip Johnston. <http://www.telegraph.co.uk/news/uknews/hs2/10870103/If-we-cant-rest-in-peace-handle-with-care.html>

"Index Of Hotel Accommodation in Central London." The London Toolkit.

<https://www.londontoolkit.com/mnu/london_hotel_acc
om.htm>

"Jack the Ripper." Wikipedia.
<https://en.wikipedia.org/wiki/Jack_the_Ripper>

"Jewel Tower." English Heritage. <http://www.english-
heritage.org.uk/visit/places/jewel-tower/>

"Jewel Tower." Wikipedia.
<https://en.wikipedia.org/wiki/Jewel_Tower>

"Kensington." Wikipedia.
<https://en.wikipedia.org/wiki/Kensington>

"Kensington Gardens." The Royal Parks.
<https://www.royalparks.org.uk/parks/kensington-
gardens>

"Kensington Gardens." Wikipedia.
<https://en.wikipedia.org/wiki/Kensington_Gardens>

"Kensington Gardens, A Royal Park." VisitLondon.com.
<http://www.visitlondon.com/things-to-do/place/433226-
kensington-gardens-a-royal-
park#QHyxAB3CBAQA3Zaq.97>

"Kew Gardens." TimeOut.
<http://www.timeout.com/london/attractions/kew-
gardens>

"Kew Gardens." Wikipedia.
<https://en.wikipedia.org/wiki/Kew_Gardens#Kew_Palac
e>

"Kings Cross." Wikipedia.
<https://en.wikipedia.org/wiki/Kings_Cross,_London>

"King's Road." VisitLondon.com.
<http://www.visitlondon.com/things-to-
do/place/29445369-kings-road#k5VDIZ5mFqBvvoey.97>

"King's Road." Wikipedia.
<https://en.wikipedia.org/wiki/King%27s_Road>

"Knightsbridge." LondonTown.
<http://www.londontown.com/LondonInformation/Shop
ping/Knightsbridge/6a71/>

"Knightsbridge." Wikipedia.
<https://en.wikipedia.org/wiki/Knightsbridge#Economy>

"London Eye." A View on Cities.
<http://www.aviewoncities.com/london/londoneye.htm>

"London Eye." Wikipedia.
<https://en.wikipedia.org/wiki/London_Eye>

"London: London Hotel Districts." TripAdvisor.
<https://www.tripadvisor.com/Travel-g186338-
c50605/London:United-
Kingdom:London.Hotel.Districts.html>

"London's 15 Best Pubs." Abbey Chase.
<http://www.fodors.com/world/europe/england/london/
experiences/news/photos/londons-15-best-pubs>

"London's best beer gardens." TimeOut.
<http://www.timeout.com/london/bars-pubs/londons-
best-beer-gardens>

"London' Best City Farms." Kate Lough.
<http://www.standard.co.uk/goingout/attractions/london
s-best-city-farms-8728644.html>

"London's Best Historical Pubs: The Ultimate Tour." Jolyon
Attwooll.
<http://www.telegraph.co.uk/travel/destinations/europe/
united-kingdom/england/london/articles/Londons-best-
historical-pubs-the-ultimate-tour/>

"London's Best Open-Air Cinemas." Afro.
<http://www.brokeinlondon.com/best-open-air-cinemas-
london/>

"London's Big Ben." VisitLondon.com.
<http://www.visitlondon.com/things-to-
do/sightseeing/london-attraction/big-
ben#wj6kQWuMUjSUQVb1.97>

"London Millenium Footbridge." WalkLondon.
<http://www.walklondon.com/london-
attractions/millennium-footbridge.htm>

"London Pub Crawl with London Gone Wild." Free Tours By Foot. <http://www.freetoursbyfoot.com/london-tours/walking-tours/london-pub-crawl-london-gone-wild/>

"London visitor numbers hit record levels." The Guardian. <https://www.theguardian.com/travel/2016/may/20/london-record-visitor-numbers-2015-31-5-million>

"London's Roman Amphiteatre." City of London. <https://www.cityoflondon.gov.uk/things-to-do/visit-the-city/attractions/guildhall-galleries/Pages/londons-roman-amphitheatre.aspx>

"Madame Tussauds." Wikipedia. <https://en.wikipedia.org/wiki/Madame_Tussauds>

"Map of St. James's Park." The Royal Parks. <https://www.royalparks.org.uk/parks/st-jamess-park/map-of-st-jamess-park>

"Millenium Bridge." A View on Cities. <http://www.aviewoncities.com/london/millenniumbridge.htm>

"Millenium Bridge, London." London Landmarks. <http://www.urban75.org/london/millennium.html>

"Museum of London." VisitLondon.com. <http://www.visitlondon.com/things-to-do/place/97363-museum-of-london#odmfs22ZX2qU65aQ.97>

"Museum of London." Wikipedia.
    <https://en.wikipedia.org/wiki/Museum_of_London>

"National Gallery." Wikipedia.
    <https://en.wikipedia.org/wiki/National_Gallery#Sainsbu
    ry_Wing_and_later_additions>

"National Maritime Museum." Lauralee Davies.
    <http://www.timeout.com/london/museums/national-
    maritime-museum>

"National Maritime Museum." Wikipedia.
    <https://en.wikipedia.org/wiki/National_Maritime_Muse
    um>

"National Maritime Museum Greenwich." VisitLondon.com.
    <http://www.visitlondon.com/things-to-do/place/450869-
    national-maritime-museum-
    greenwich#bMhkTwXVZqGIdCRt.97>

"National Portrait Gallery." LondonTown.
    <http://www.londontown.com/LondonInformation/Attra
    ction/National_Portrait_Gallery/3cee/>

"National Portrait Gallery." The Art Fund.
    <https://www.artfund.org/what-to-see/museums-and-
    galleries/national-portrait-gallery>

"National Portrait Gallery." VisitLondon.com.
    <http://www.visitlondon.com/things-to-do/place/95587-
    national-portrait-gallery#xA5aZoxPVlqmWIgB.97>

"National Portrait Gallery, London." Wikipedia.
 <https://en.wikipedia.org/wiki/National_Portrait_Gallery
 ,_London>

"Natural History Museum." Art Fund.
 <https://www.artfund.org/what-to-see/museums-and-
 galleries/natural-history-museum>

"Natural History Museum." LondonTown.
 <http://www.londontown.com/LondonInformation/Attra
 ction/Natural_History_Museum/aab8/>

"Natural History Museum." Lonely Planet.
 <http://www.lonelyplanet.com/england/london/sights/m
 useums-galleries/natural-history-museum>

"Natural History Museum, London." Wikipedia.
 <https://en.wikipedia.org/wiki/Natural_History_Museu
 m,_London>

"Open-air theatre in London." Time Out London Theatre.
 <http://www.timeout.com/london/theatre/open-air-
 theatre-in-london>

"Outdoor cinema in London." Cath Clarke.
 <http://www.timeout.com/london/film/outdoor-cinema-
 in-london>

"Oxford Street shops." Timeout.
 <http://www.timeout.com/london/shopping/oxford-
 street-shops>

"Oxford Street." VisitLondon.com.
<http://www.visitlondon.com/things-to-do/place/5042973-oxford-street#xyOPxmazjBpZZ4Xb.97>

"Oxford Street." Wikipedia.
<https://en.wikipedia.org/wiki/Oxford_Street>

"Paddington." Wikipedia.
<https://en.wikipedia.org/wiki/Paddington>

"Palace of Westminster." Wikipedia.
<https://en.wikipedia.org/wiki/Palace_of_Westminster>

"Piccadilly Circus." A View on Cities.
<http://www.aviewoncities.com/london/piccadillycircus.htm>

"Piccadilly Circus." Wikipedia.
<https://en.wikipedia.org/wiki/Piccadilly_Circus>

"Pubs in London: What to Expect." Melanie Waldman.
<http://www.londonlogue.com/featured-articles/pubs-in-london-what-to-expect-and-how-to-find-them.html>

"Queen Elizabeth's Hunting Lodge." Natalie.
<http://onthetudortrail.com/Blog/2011/06/10/queen-elizabeths-hunting-lodge/>

"Queen Elizabeth's Hunting Lodge." VisitLondon.com.
<http://www.visitlondon.com/things-to-do/place/69004-queen-elizabeths-hunting-lodge#PR5sV1gJYySoubc5.97>

"Queen Elizabeth's Hunting Lodge." Wikipedia.
    <https://en.wikipedia.org/wiki/Queen_Elizabeth%27s_H
    unting_Lodge>

"Queen Elizabeth's Hunting Lodge/The View." Visit Essex.
    <http://www.visitessex.com/thedms.aspx?dms=3&venue
    =0248457>

"Queen's Guard." Wikipedia.
    <https://en.wikipedia.org/wiki/Queen%27s_Guard#Chan
    ging_the_Queen.27s_Life_Guard>

"Record-breaking number of tourists in London in 2013."
    BBC News. <http://www.bbc.com/news/uk-england-
    london-27323755>

"Regent Street." VisitLondon.com.
    <http://www.visitlondon.com/things-to-do/place/64061-
    regent-street#itKb7xjECLUluw5R.97>

"Regent Street." Wikipedia.
    <https://en.wikipedia.org/wiki/Regent_Street#Crown_Est
    ate_redevelopment>

"Regent's Park Open Air Threatre." LondonTheatre.co.uk.
    <https://www.londontheatre.co.uk/theatres/regents-park-
    open-air-theatre>

"Regent's Park Open Air Theatre." VisitLondon.com.
    <http://www.visitlondon.com/things-to-do/place/279800-
    regents-park-open-air-theatre#vxQXvxFofQDdEFlV.97>

"Regent's Park Open Air Theatre." Wikipedia.
<https://en.wikipedia.org/wiki/Regent%27s_Park_Open_
Air_Theatre>

"Restaurants near Bond Street." TripAdvisor.
<https://www.tripadvisor.com.ph/RestaurantsNear-
g186338-d188711-Bond_Street-London_England.html>

"Royal Botanic Gardens, Kew." VisitLondon.com.
<http://www.visitlondon.com/things-to-do/place/58711-
royal-botanic-gardens-kew#T4SATo5vPd0bC1GL.97>

"Royal Mews." VisitBritain.
<https://www.visitbritainshop.com/world/the-royal-
mews/>

"Royal Mews." VisitLondon.com.
<http://www.visitlondon.com/things-to-do/place/478563-
royal-mews#EIDWEHMA4wMrMYSe.97>

"Royal Mews." Wikipedia.
<https://en.wikipedia.org/wiki/Royal_Mews>

"Science Museum." TimeOut.
<http://www.timeout.com/london/museums/science-
museum>

"Science Museum." VisitLondon.com.
<http://www.visitlondon.com/things-to-do/place/52747-
science-museum#gJxY6JErKKXvBpbv.97>

"Science Museum, London." Wikipedia.
<https://en.wikipedia.org/wiki/Science_Museum,_Londo
n#Location>

"Science Museum (London)." Wikipedia.
<https://simple.wikipedia.org/wiki/Science_Museum_(Lo
ndon)>

"Sea Life London Aquarium." VisitLondon.com.
<http://www.visitlondon.com/things-to-do/place/117322-
sea-life-london-aquarium#X3b8p8S6P6ytgEMQ.97>

"Sea Life London Aquarium." Wikipedia.
<https://en.wikipedia.org/wiki/Sea_Life_London_Aquari
um>

"See London by Night." Live Guided Tours.
<http://seelondonbynight.com/>

"Shakespeare's Globe." Wikipedia.
<https://en.wikipedia.org/wiki/Shakespeare%27s_Globe>

"Sherlock Holmes Museum." Wikipedia.
<https://en.wikipedia.org/wiki/Sherlock_Holmes_Museu
m>

"Shopping in Knightsbridge." LondonTown.
<http://www.londontown.com/NearByShopping/Shoppi
ng/Directory/Areas/Knightsbridge/Shopping/Shopping-
near-Knightsbridge/>

"Sightseeing Times & Prices." St. Paul's Cathedral. <https://www.stpauls.co.uk/visits/visits/sightseeing-times-prices>

"Stars in Their Eyes." The New Hamptonian. <http://www.hampsteadvillagelondon.com/blog/stars-in-their-eyes/>

"St. James's Park." A View on Cities. <http://www.aviewoncities.com/london/stjamespark.htm>

"St. James's Park." The Royal Parks Foundation. <http://www.supporttheroyalparks.org/visit_the_parks/st_jamess_park>

"St. James's Park." Wikipedia. <https://en.wikipedia.org/wiki/St_James%27s_Park>

"St. Pancras Old Church." Wikipedia. <https://en.wikipedia.org/wiki/St_Pancras_Old_Church>

"St. Paul's Cathedral." A View on Cities. <http://www.aviewoncities.com/london/stpaulscathedral.htm>

"St. Paul's Cathedral." Wikipedia. <https://en.wikipedia.org/wiki/St_Paul%27s_Cathedral>

"Tate Britain." Graphiq. <http://museums.wanderbat.com/l/709/Tate-Britain>

"Tate Britain." Tate. <http://www.tate.org.uk/visit/tate-britain>

"Tate Britain." Wikipedia. <https://en.wikipedia.org/wiki/Tate_Britain>

"Tate Modern." Lonely Planet. <http://www.lonelyplanet.com/england/london/sights/museums-galleries/tate-modern>

"Tate Modern." VisitLondon.com. <http://www.visitlondon.com/things-to-do/place/344410-tate-modern#overview#OMJocqiAtwRJGUvx.97>

"Tate Modern." Wikipedia. <https://en.wikipedia.org/wiki/Tate_Modern>

"Thames Barrier Information Centre." VisitLondon.com. <http://www.visitlondon.com/things-to-do/place/26941-thames-barrier-information-centre#6bi1X5YJMvT4Rqvy.97>

"The 10 Best Restaurants in London's Knightsbridge." Richard Vines. <http://www.bloomberg.com/news/articles/2015-02-12/the-10-best-restaurants-in-london-s-knightsbridge>

"The Best Comedy Clubs in London." TimeOut. <http://www.timeout.com/london/comedy/the-best-comedy-clubs-in-london-1>

"The Best Free Comedy in London." TimeOut. <http://www.timeout.com/london/comedy/the-best-free-comedy-in-london>

"The Hardy Tree." Atlas Obscura. <http://www.atlasobscura.com/places/the-hardy-tree>

"The Jewel Tower 1365." Living Heritage. <http://www.parliament.uk/about/living-heritage/building/palace/estatehistory/the-middle-ages/jewel-tower/>

"The Jewel Tower: A Hidden Gem." Free Tours By Foot. <http://www.freetoursbyfoot.com/jewel-tower-hidden-gem/>

"The King's Road." LondonTown. <http://www.londontown.com/LondonInformation/Shopping/The_Kings_Road/7419/>

"The London Eye." David Coleman. <https://havecamerawilltravel.com/london-eye/>

"The Millenium Bridge." VisitLondon.com. <http://www.visitlondon.com/things-to-do/place/442404-millennium-bridge#eVquGwA1ABeWfScf.97>

"The National Gallery, London." Google Arts & Culture. <https://www.google.com/culturalinstitute/beta/partner/the-national-gallery-london>

"The new Tate Modern is infuriating and exhilarating in equal measure - review." Mark Hudson. <http://www.telegraph.co.uk/art/what-to-see/the-new-tate-modern-is-infuriating-and-exhilarating-in-equal-mea/>

"The Original Camden Pub Crawl." Undiscovered London. <https://www.undiscoveredlondon.com/things-to-do/nightlife/pub-crawls/camden-pub-crawl/>

"The Pet Cemetery of Hyde Park." londoninsight. <https://londoninsight.wordpress.com/2010/10/06/pet-cemetery-hyde-park/>

"The Shard." Wikipedia. <https://en.wikipedia.org/wiki/The_Shard>

"The Sherlock Holmes." Wikipedia. <https://en.wikipedia.org/wiki/The_Sherlock_Holmes>

"The Sherlock Holmes Pub." Atlas Obscura. <http://www.atlasobscura.com/places/the-sherlock-holmes-pub>

"The ten best shops on Regent Street." Katie Rosseinsky. <http://www.timeout.com/london/shopping/the-ten-best-shops-on-regent-street>

"The Thames Barrier." Royal Geographical Society. <https://21stcenturychallenges.org/the-thames-barrier/>

"The Tower of London." Kenndi-1066."
<https://bossieraim.wikispaces.com/The+Tower+of+Lond
on>

"The Ultimate Guide: Where to Stay in London." Young
Rubbish.
<http://www.youngrubbish.com/2015/03/Ultimate-
Guide-Where-to-Stay-London.html>

"The Victorian Pet Cemetery of Hyde Park." Matt Gedge.
<https://funlondontours.com/news/victorian-pet-
cemetery-hyde-park>

"The View from the Shard." Wikipedia.
<https://en.wikipedia.org/wiki/The_View_from_the_Shar
d>

"Things To Do In Camden Town." VisitLondon.com.
<http://www.visitlondon.com/discover-london/london-
areas/central/camden-town#D9YogWAll4xTuQ22.97>

"Things to Take to London." Benna Crawford.
<http://traveltips.usatoday.com/things-london-
43042.html>

"Top 10 best stores on the King's Road." Emily Scrivener.
<http://www.globalblue.com/destinations/uk/top-10-
best-stores-on-the-kings-road/>

"Top 10 Camden." VisitLondon.com.
<http://www.visitlondon.com/discover-london/london-
areas/central/camden-top-10#Grl3PFTtp5TPdymy.97>

"Top 10 Places to go shopping in Knightsbridge." City Marque. <https://www.citymarque.com/top-10-places-to-go-shopping-in-knightsbridge/>

"Top 10 Unique London Attractions Off the Tourist Track." Londontopia. <http://londontopia.net/travel/top-10-unique-london-attractions-off-the-tourist-track/>

"Top Ten Things To Do In London At Night." Free Tours By Foot. <http://www.freetoursbyfoot.com/top-ten-things-london-night/>

"Tower Bridge." Wikipedia. <https://en.wikipedia.org/wiki/Tower_Bridge>

"Tower Bridge: fascinating facts and figures." Oliver Smith. <http://www.telegraph.co.uk/travel/destinations/europe/united-kingdom/england/london/south-east/london-bridge/articles/Tower-Bridge-fascinating-facts-and-figures/>

"Tower of London." Lonely Planet. <http://www.lonelyplanet.com/england/london/sights/castles-palaces-mansions/tower-london>

"Tower of London." UNESCO. <http://whc.unesco.org/en/list/488>

"Tower of London." Wikipedia. <https://en.wikipedia.org/wiki/Tower_of_London>

"Tower of London/Ceremony of the Keys." ChangingGuard.com. <http://changing-guard.com/ceremony-of-the-keys.html>

"Tower Ravens." Ben Johnson. <http://www.historic-uk.com/HistoryMagazine/DestinationsUK/Tower-Ravens/>

"Trafalgar Square." A view on Cities. <http://www.aviewoncities.com/london/trafalgarsquare.htm>

"Trafalgar Square." LondonTown. <http://www.londontown.com/LondonInformation/Attraction/Trafalgar_Square/f106/>

"Trafalgar Square." Lonely Planet. <http://www.lonelyplanet.com/england/london/sights/squares-plazas/trafalgar-square>

"Trafalgar Square Sights." About Travel. <http://golondon.about.com/od/thingstodoinlondon/ss/trafalgarsquare.htm>

"Victoria, London." Wikipedia. <https://en.wikipedia.org/wiki/Victoria,_London>

"Victoria and Albert Museum." Wikipedia. <https://en.wikipedia.org/wiki/Victoria_and_Albert_Museum>

"Victoria & Albert Museum, London: the director's guide." John O'Ceallaigh. <http://www.telegraph.co.uk/luxury/travel/67851/victoria-and-albert-museum-london-guide-director-tips-martin-roth.html>

"Victoria Visitor Briefing." The London Toolkit." <https://www.londontoolkit.com/accommodation/victoria_briefing.htm>

"Visit Hampton Court Palace with The London Pass." The London Pass. <https://www.londonpass.com/london-attractions/hampton-court-palace.html>

"Visit Westminster Abbey for Free - Save £20!" The London Pass. <https://www.londonpass.com/london-attractions/westminster-abbey.html>

"Visitor Tickets." Transport for London. <https://visitorshop.tfl.gov.uk/>

"Waterloo, London." Wikipedia. <https://en.wikipedia.org/wiki/Waterloo,_London>

"Weather and Seasons." Education UK. <http://www.educationuk.org/global/articles/weather-and-seasons/>

"Welcome to Dennis Severs' House." Dennis Severs' House. <http://www.dennissevershouse.co.uk/>

"West End." Wikipedia.
<https://en.wikipedia.org/wiki/West_End_of_London>

"West End Theatre." Wikipedia.
<https://en.wikipedia.org/wiki/West_End_theatre>

"Westfield London." Wikipedia.
<https://en.wikipedia.org/wiki/Westfield_London>

"Westfield London and Westfield Stratford."
VisitLondon.com. <http://www.visitlondon.com/things-
to-do/shopping/westfield#pAOL1SgzxbDSQakp.97>

"Westfield Stratford City." Wikipedia.
<https://en.wikipedia.org/wiki/Westfield_Stratford_City>

"Westminster Abbey." VisitLondon.com.
<http://www.visitlondon.com/things-to-do/place/610825-
westminster-abbey#c8HQBlIo2CzjpdtR.97>

"Westminster Abbey." Wikipedia.
<https://en.wikipedia.org/wiki/Westminster_Abbey>

"What You Need To Know Before Traveling to England."
Halle Eavelyn. <http://www.huffingtonpost.com/halle-
eavelyn/england-what-you-need-to-
know_b_4920852.html>

"Where to see bats in Greater London." London Bat Group.
<http://www.londonbats.org.uk/wherebat.htm>

"Which Are the Best London Night Tours?" Free Tours By Foot. <http://www.freetoursbyfoot.com/which-are-the-best-london-night-tours/>

"Yeoman Warders." Wikipedia. <https://en.wikipedia.org/wiki/Yeomen_Warders>

"Your Guide To The Best Live Music Venues in London." Louise Johnston. <https://lovin.ie/travel-food/cities/london/your-guide-to-the-best-live-music-venues-in-london>

Feeding Baby
Cynthia Cherry
978-1941070000

Axolotl
Lolly Brown
978-0989658430

Dysautonomia, POTS
Syndrome
Frederick Earlstein
978-0989658485

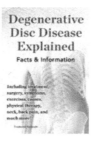

Degenerative Disc
Disease Explained
Frederick Earlstein
978-0989658485

Sinusitis, Hay Fever,
Allergic Rhinitis Explained
Frederick Earlstein
978-1941070024

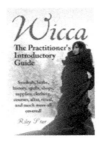

Wicca
Riley Star
978-1941070130

Zombie Apocalypse
Rex Cutty
978-1941070154

Capybara
Lolly Brown
978-1941070062

Eels As Pets
Lolly Brown
978-1941070167

Scabies and Lice Explained
Frederick Earlstein
978-1941070017

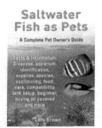

Saltwater Fish As Pets
Lolly Brown
978-0989658461

Torticollis Explained
Frederick Earlstein
978-1941070055

Kennel Cough
Lolly Brown
978-0989658409

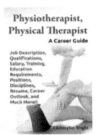

Physiotherapist, Physical
Therapist
Christopher Wright
978-0989658492

Rats, Mice, and Dormice
As Pets
Lolly Brown
978-1941070079

Wallaby and Wallaroo Care
Lolly Brown
978-1941070031

Bodybuilding Supplements
Explained
Jon Shelton
978-1941070239

Demonology
Riley Star
978-19401070314

Pigeon Racing
Lolly Brown
978-1941070307

Dwarf Hamster
Lolly Brown
978-1941070390

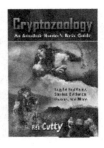

Cryptozoology
Rex Cutty
978-1941070406

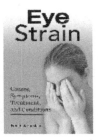

Eye Strain
Frederick Earlstein
978-1941070369

Inez The Miniature Elephant
Asher Ray
978-1941070353

Vampire Apocalypse
Rex Cutty
978-1941070321